# THE VALLEY ROAD

ILLUSTRATED BY MARGARET LOWENGRUND

# The Valley Road

## BY FAY INGALLS

CLEVELAND AND NEW YORK

THE WORLD PUBLISHING COMPANY

*Published by* THE WORLD PUBLISHING COMPANY

2231 WEST 110TH STREET · CLEVELAND 2 · OHIO

*First published March 1949*
*Second printing October 1949*

TO

# R. H. I.

*without whose sympathetic understanding
and patience this story could not have
existed or been told*

# Contents

# Contents

# THE VALLEY ROAD

# *1. The Indians Travel the Road*

FOR MORE than half a century I have known and loved that portion of the higher Alleghany Mountains which comprises the Counties of Bath and Highland in Virginia and the neighboring ones across the line in West Virginia. Although there are rugged peaks and deep ravines, it is essentially a peaceful, gentle land. The landscape has a feminine charm, with its high hills, buttressed by rounded shoulders, sweeping smoothly down to the valleys. It bespeaks of fertility and life, with its wooded hillsides overlooking green pastures. There are no rocky crags of awe-inspiring majesty but, to compensate, promise of life in its fullness.  A grizzled mountaineer gave me a glimpse of what it was like before men came to exploit it.  Shooting grouse in West Virginia, just across the state line, when there were no National Forest trails, I had prevailed on the owner of a small clearing on the top of Alleghany Mountain to show me where the birds were and how to get about.  He knew the country and the haunts of game but had one troubling fault; although apparently twice my age, he did not seem to feel the difference in going up or down hill to get from here to there.  On one of his short cuts I stopped for breath and leaning against a huge moss-covered stump, remarked, "This must have been a wonderful country before trees such as this were cut."

"It sure was," he replied.  "You couldn't feel the ground for the moss and you couldn't see the sun for the trees, and game was everywhere."

Through this country there is a valley down which runs a road, now paved macadam but first a game trail, then an Indian path and later part of the highroad used by pioneers moving from eastern Virginia into the virgin lands of the west.  The road meanders over the Valley floor, most of the way passing through fertile farming land, rising at times to cross the shoulders jutting out from Warm Springs Mountain and dipping down at the gaps through which the streams flow.  It is tapped near Warm Springs by the highway which crosses the pass from the east at that point.

Along this road the stream of life has been flowing since time immemorial.  When it was but a game trail it went through a mighty forest, one of the greatest temperate zone stretches of woodland on the continent of North America.  It was of wondrous variety, an area where southern and northern flora met, the valley floor claiming the tenderer species and the heights the hardier northern. Today there is a difference of two weeks in the progress of the seasons between the Valley floor and the ridges. Except on the heights the Valley is sheltered from high winds, the frequent streams checked lightning-kindled fires, and the trees grew to giant proportions. The cycle of growth through geological ages created a soil of rich fertility, the roots reaching for nourishment beneath the surface, breaking down the chemicals in the rocks and decaying leaves and fallen age-killed trees forming humus. Down the road went buffalo, white-tailed deer, a host of smaller herbage-eating animals and in their wake the predators. That there were immense numbers of game animals can be deduced from names given to portions of this road by early settlers; it left the Shenandoah Valley through Buffalo Gap, soon crossed the Cowpasture, Calf Pasture and Bullpasture Rivers, where these pioneers found herds of buffaloes, and then plunged into the heart of the mountains through Panther Gap.

The Indians followed game up and down the road. When they came to the Valley, however, they found another attraction in the Warm Springs, which were ultimately the reason for the white man's coming. There is a quaint legend of how the first Indian found the springs, published by a Mr. Otis of Boston, in the 1833 issue of the *Southern Literary Messenger*, as he heard it from the keeper of the Baths at Warm Springs:

"A young Indian, more than two centuries ago, was coming from the western valley of the great Appalachian Mountains, toward the waters of the East, that opened into the beautiful bay whose branches touch the strands of some of the mightiest marts of a nation that was not then in existence. He had never trodden that path before, and nothing but the pride of youth, which would not brook that his brethren of other tribes should triumph over him as their inferior in adventure, had sustained his manly heart so far; for he had come, since the rising sun first touched that day the mighty peaks of the Alleghanies, from the vales that lay at their feet on the west. He was going to carry the voice and vote of a powerful nation to the council-fire that was kindling on the banks of the great water, and he felt shame at the recurrence of the idea that the place of the young Appalachian Leopard could be vacant. But the night winds beat coldly around him, and the way was dark. There had been rains, and the earth was damp and swampy; and no grass, or fern, or heather, was at hand with which to make a bed in the bosom of the valley where he stood. He had not strength to climb the near range of mountains that drew up their summits before, as if to shut out all hopes that he could accomplish his ardent desire. Weary, dispirited, and ready to despair, he came suddenly upon an open space among the low underwood that covered the valley where he was wandering, and upon looking narrowly he observed that it was filled with water. He could see the clear reflection of the bright evening star that was just declining to her rest, and that was peeping into the fountain,

> 'Like a bride full of blushes, just lingering to take
> A last look in her mirror, at night, ere she goes.'

"By this translucent reflection, he could perceive that the water was clear, and its depth he could discern by the pebbles that glistened in the starlight from the bottom. He saw, too, that the water was continually flowing off, and supplying a stream that ran rippling away among the roots of the oaks that surrounded the spot; and as he stooped to taste the liquid element, he found it warm, as if inviting him to relax his chilled limbs by bathing in its tepid bosom.

"He laid aside his bow and quiver, unstrung his pouch from his brawny shoulder, took off his moccasins, and plunged in. A new life invigorated his wearied spirit; new strength seemed given to his almost rigid nerves; he swam, he dived, he lay prostrate upon the genial waves in a sort of dreaming ecstasy of delight; and when the first dawn of day broke over the rock-crowned hill, at the foot of which the Spring of Strength lay enshrined, the young Leopard came forth from his watery couch, and strode proudly up the mountain 'where path there was none'.

"He was a 'young giant rejoicing to run his course.' Full of new fire and vigor, he manfully sped his way; and upon the eve of that day, when the chiefs and the sons of chiefs were seated around the solemn council-fire, no one of them all was found more graceful in address, more commanding in manner, more pleasing in look, and sagacious in policy, than the young Appalachian Leopard who bathed in the 'Spring of Strength'."

Whether or not this was the first Indian to find the springs, there is no question but that they bathed in both the Warm and the Hot Springs. So far as can be determined there never was a permanent Indian settlement in the Valley. It was frequently visited by the Tidewater tribes. Annually these went on extended hunting expeditions and there seems to have been a regular thoroughfare up the Potomac and down the James, or vice versa. The headwaters of both these rivers are in Highland County about forty miles north of Hot Springs, and the distance between canoeable water of the two perhaps sixty miles.

It is obvious that the Indians spent considerable time camping hereabout while on these treks. There is usually a flat on the up-river bank where tributary streams enter the Jackson or the Cowpasture, and on these is extensive evidence of kitchen middens. Dr. E. Reinhold Rogers, Rector of St. Luke's Episcopal Church, at Hot Springs, had a fine collection of Indian artifacts, many of which were collected from these camp sites. The only evidences of a more permanent Indian population are the mounds which have given the name to one of the riding trails, The Indian Fort Trail. To the best of my knowledge and belief these have never been investigated. Their location on the end of a long ridge makes it seem unlikely that they were military works, as locally reputed. Indian mounds are well known in other parts and these are probably but another instance of some phase of Indian life not entirely deciphered.

It is said that when several Indian tribes settled in territory where there was plenty of game, with good hunting grounds adjacent to all, it was their custom to designate such hunting grounds as sanctuaries and all feuds or incidental scalp taking were taboo while on hunting expeditions. At all events it seems to be true that these mountains never echoed the war cries, at least until the white man came. Many in recent years have called the Warm Springs Valley "The Peaceful Valley." Perhaps the Indians, looking at the gently rolling mountains, the brooks and forests, may have been moved by the same emotions felt by moderns, and the truce was not entirely utilitarian.

# 2. *The First Homestead*

IT IS not known when the first white man came to the
Valley. The story is told that the springs were discovered by General Andrew Lewis, who, fleeing from
the Indians, hid in the heavy bushes about them. This
makes a good story but it won't stand up, for Andrew
Lewis was born in 1720, and in 1727 Robert and Willam
Lewis, James Mills, Robert Brooke, Jr., Beverly Robinson
and William Lynn petitioned the Governor and Council
for a grant of land along the Cowpasture River. Records
are not clear as to whether a grant was forthcoming as

7

requested but obviously the country was known and in
fact there were squatters along the river at that time.
Although the early settlers were blocked for a time by the
Warm Springs Mountain, it is hardly possible that the
springs were not discovered until Andrew was old enough
to be fighting Indians.    In 1743 leave was granted to
Andrew Lewis and three others to take up fifty thousand
acres of land in the Jackson and Cowpasture Valleys but
whether or not this grant had any connection with the
petition of 1720 is not known.    In 1751 the first actual title
to land in the Valley was surveyed, consisting of 140
acres at Warm Springs, to John Lewis (son of Andrew or
Thomas Lewis) and John Lewis, Jr. Eventually this holding of the Lewises was extended until at one time they
were the owners of the Warm Springs tract of about
1,700 acres, which through many hands, has remained
practically intact to the present time, the last owners
being Virginia Hot Springs, Inc.

That there was a considerable population in the
Valley in 1755 is unquestioned, and by 1800 Warm Springs
was well established as a resort.    In Rev. Hugh Mc-
Fadden's diary we find a note that while at Warm Springs,
on July 16, 1755, the news of Braddock's defeat was
received, creating panic among the inhabitants.

It was in 1755 that Washington established Fort
Dinwiddie on the Jackson River, about a mile north of
Fassifern where the Huntersville Pike (now prosaically
Route 39) crosses the river. Washington seems to have
regarded this fort as a major point in the line of defenses
he designed against the Indians, and there are frequent
references to it in his writings. If he ever visited the Valley
there is no record of such a visit. All traces of this fort are
long ago gone. It was said to have been on a bluff, with an

underground passage down to the river, but this, too, has been lost.

Bath County was carved out of Augusta County, which then included the State of Kentucky, and Warm Springs selected as the county seat. The first term of court was held in the home of the widow of John Lewis, at Warm Springs, on May 10, 1791. This first court fixed the "Rates of Liquor, Stableage (sic), Fodder and Pastorage (sic) to be paid at the several ordinarys in this county in the ensuing year."

Somewhat later, in 1817 to be exact, there was a proceeding before the court which shows that troubles with price controls are not so new as some may think. John Fry, who kept the tavern at Warm Springs, and Hezekiah Dagge, who presided over that at Hot Springs, were indicted for breach of these rates. At the same term rates for the following year were fixed. Some of these prices are interesting:

| | |
|---|---|
| For Breakfast | 25 cents (all sic) |
| For Dinner | 37 & ½ cents |
| For Supper | 25 cents |
| For Whiskey (common) | 12 ½ cents |
| Lodging, per night | 12 ½ cents |
| Madeira and Claret Wine | 25 cts. pr. qt. |

At the 1791 term of court an advertisement was authorized for the construction of a permanent courthouse, and the appropriation for architect's fees was the princely sum of $3. I cannot find where this was located but sometime early in the next century a brick courthouse was built, which is now the Warm Springs Inn. A few years ago an architect friend of the writer looked at the old building, the little clerk's office to the north and the gaol behind it, exclaiming, "This is the most perfect example of good colonial architecture I have ever seen." Imagining it without the gewgaws and porches which have since been tacked on, you can see what he meant.

This courthouse served its purpose until early in the twentieth century, when it was sold by the county and the present brick and stucco monstrosity, about a mile to the south, built.

Before the old courthouse finally became an inn it had one burst of glory. The motion picture "Tol'able David" was filmed on location there. It was quite an event in the Valley when the troupe descended to make the picture—such things were more of a novelty then than they are today. It was a good picture and, as I recall it, the local color true. One scene, where the hero, as a boy, catches trout by tickling them, was scoffed at by the untutored. Some fifteen years later it became necessary to transfer trout from one pool to another at the Cascades. Rocks and uneven bottom made it impossible to use a seine effectively but one of the men, born and bred in the mountains, did the job by running his hand under the ledge where the trout sought refuge and one after another flicking them out.

The old gaol is worth seeing. The walls are of brick and feet, rather than inches, thick. There is a huge oaken door and somehow the prisoners were allowed jackknives and covered the door with bas-relief. These carvings are as naturalistic and crude as anything Gauguin ever perpetrated.

The Lewis family led the pioneering into the Valley but with the acquisition of the first legal title to the Warm Springs tract in 1751 their drive seems to have stopped. True the family retained control of the Warm for a long time but when the Hot Springs tract was surveyed and patented a few years later a new name came into the picture and we find that this patent was issued to Andrew and Thomas Lewis in company with Thomas Bullitt, who is supposed to have built the first Homestead at Hot Springs about 1756. Apparently in the succeeding years Bullitt was the moving spirit at Hot Springs.

How Thomas Bullitt happened to come to Hot Springs cannot be said with much certainty today. About ten years ago a gentleman, a clergyman incidentally, who said he was a great-great-grandson of Cuthbert Bullitt, gave his version of the family history. There are a few pegs, in the way of recorded deeds and the like, on which to hang the fabric of this story and in the main it is probably true as told, but when submitted to another of the present generation of Bullitts, it was scoffed at. Anyway, here it is.

Thomas Bullitt was the son of one James Bullitt, who had settled in Maryland and moved to Fauquier County, Virginia. He fought as an officer in various pre-Revolutionary Indian wars and it is a fair assumption that while doing so met Andrew Lewis, who had attained sufficient military prominence so that when the Continental Army was organized his friends thought he should have been named Commander-in-Chief instead of Washington. The pay of these colonial officers was skimpy and it was customary to reward their services by grants of unsettled western lands. The most famous of the grants is, of course, that to Washington. Bullitt, who seems to have served with some distinction, was eligible for such a grant and what more natural than that he should join up with the Lewises, already established in the Valley.

The partnership with the Lewises did not last long and was formally dissolved in 1769, although the two families remained closely allied and the Lewises kept their connection with Warm Springs. Thomas Bullitt early associated his brother Cuthbert with his venture but Cuthbert moved on to Kentucky, where he had a distinguished career. However, that the Bullitt family retained a link with the Valley is shown by the fact that we find John Fry proprietor of the Warm in the 1830's, and Fry had married a daughter of Cuthbert Bullitt, who became the great-grandmother of my informant.

As the story goes, the Bullitts were not overly pleased with their estate in the deep mountains. They had expected to establish a plantation similar to those in Tidewater Virginia but discovered, in spite of the glowing accounts of the fertility of the land with which the Lewises embellished their various petitions for land grants, that the land was too broken up and difficulties of transportation too great for plantation agriculture. This probably discouraged Cuthbert Bullitt and led to his moving farther west. Thomas Bullitt made a brave effort to live up to the traditions of Eastern Virginia, and we find him advertising that certain horses of noted racing breed would be sold in the summer at the "Springs." The assumption is that this sale was to provide for his debts if anything should happen to him on a visit he then contemplated to Kentucky.

It is said that Thomas Bullitt extended hospitality to all comers, not only to casual travelers but to the increasing numbers who wanted to bathe in the waters; this became irksome and Bullitt proposed to his slaves that they erect a tavern from materials he would furnish and take compensation for the hospitality provided, which he considered beneath his dignity. This story is a bit apocryphal as in the petition for the patent to Bullitt and the Lewises there was a stipulation that, if granted, they would erect a hotel for the accommodation of visitors and "properly stock it with wines, etc." At all events, this hotel was built prior to 1766 and called The Homestead. We don't know what sort of building Bullitt's slaves erected but it seems to have remained substantially unchanged for around seventy-five years. During this time development of the Valley was almost entirely confined to Warm Springs and the records of Hot Springs are few and far between, mostly notes by travelers, who seemed to be chiefly impressed with the crudity of accommodations and meagreness of the fare.

Thomas Bullitt died without marrying, leaving his Hot Springs properties to his brother, Cuthbert. Cuthbert, or his estate, soon sold these properties and from that time on until 1832 there seems to have been absentee ownership.

In 1825 a rather remarkable man settled in the Valley, Thomas Goode, a physician, who was to be responsible for the real beginnings of Hot Springs as a Spa. By 1832 Dr. Goode had acquired ownership of the Hot Springs property and seems to have prospered in spite of the primitive plant he took over. The dates when more ample and improved bathhouses were added are unknown but it is established that by 1837 he was prescribing the "Spout Bath," which in its essentials is still the foundation of spa treatments at The Homestead. By 1846 he was able to announce the opening of a "Modern Hotel" which he called The Homestead after its predecessor. This was on the site of the present Homestead and some of the framing from that building was incorporated in the remodeled Homestead in 1891, later destroyed in the fire of 1901. Of the other buildings, bathhouses, cabins and the like, which he constructed, all but one have been razed to make room for developments.

The lone survival is the bandstand on the hill above the
tennis courts, which was put up some time before 1847,
the exact date indeterminable.

Goode was certainly an intelligent man and well
educated for his day. We have most of our knowledge of
him from a pamphlet he published in 1846, just after the
opening of his modern hotel. His prosperity was beginning
to cut in on other spas and this pamphlet was written by
him to refute what he felt were slurring remarks, in print
and otherwise, by Burke, who was then a physician at
White Sulphur. To justify his scientific standing Goode
recounted his personal history, stating that he had studied
medicine for five years, attended three "full courses of
medical lectures" in Philadelphia and one in Edinburgh,
attended practice at the Pennsylvania Hospital for two
years, the Infirmary in Edinburgh for one, and graduated
in Philadelphia in 1811. From the first Goode stressed
Hot Springs as a Spa. While in his circulars and letters
he emphasized the modernness and comfort of his establishment, he seems to have accepted the superiority of the
Warm, White Sulphur and Old Sweet Springs for the gay
social whirl. In this book of 1846 he published some most
extraordinary letters as testimonials to the efficacy of the
waters of Hot Springs and seemed to take pleasure in those
from visitors who obtained benefit after failure at other
springs. Reading between the lines, one is led to suspect
that perhaps one reason for such failure was that so-
journers at the White, Old Sweet and the Warm did not
pursue a regime, aside from the drinking of the waters
and bathing, which was conducive to regaining health.

One with modern ideas of medicine marvels at these
testimonials. Goode insisted that the baths at Hot
Springs were truly a panacea. Even the names of the

diseases listed as curable now sound strange. More frequently than any other we find references to hepatitis,
but the whole gamut was covered, rheumatism and gout,
of course, also dysentery, phthisis, dropsy, cholera, bilious
fever, jaundice, deafness, loss of voice, uterine disorders
dyspepsia, bilious intermittent fever and what not. It
seemed to rankle with Goode that he was accused of
overcharging, and he gives his rates: For $3 he would
advise any invalid, and for $5 would continue to give
advice while the patient was at Hot Springs. He had a
special exemption for clergymen, who were treated free.

It is easy to forget how great a change has come in
the science of medicine since 1846. Within the decade
before and after that date a number of books were published on the subject of mineral springs and on those of
Virginia in particular. While much in these seems as
ridiculous as some of Goode's testimonials, there is quite
a bit of common sense, such as the premise that excessive
use of alcohol and dissipation were incompatible with
the regime at the Spa and might engender serious consequences. Some of these writers went so far as to say
that, aside from the question of the value of such springs
for their chemical content, bathing or exercising in a
warm bath was beneficial, which is much the attitude
physicians take today.

At all events the spas of Virginia had a boom about this
time. Where Goode got his figures no one can say, but in
1846 he estimated that 8,000 people came for treatment
to spas within a radius of forty miles of Hot Springs.
As none of these places could take guests except in
summer it must have been a pretty busy time for all
concerned. The highways could not have been better
than when I first knew them in the 1890's, and the dis-

comforts of these people, suffering from the aches and
pains for which spa treatments have always been considered particularly efficacious, must have been a night-
mare.

Dr. Goode apparently fell foul of a difficulty which
has plagued every development in the Valley, the provision of a sufficient sanitary water supply.   Mineral
springs are unsatisfactory for such a purpose and ultimately The Homestead had to spend over half a million
dollars before the problem was solved.  Goode's solution
was interesting.  There is a large spring, called the "Old
Dairy Spring," up the road which crosses the seventeenth
fairway of the Homestead course, a little over a mile from
The Homestead and Goode brought the water down from
this through wooden pipes.  These were made by boring
holes about three inches in diameter longitudinally
through oak logs.  One end of the log was tapered and
the other enlarged so that the tapered end of one log
could be driven into a tight joint with the next.  This
water supply was in use for fifty years.  Just a few years
ago men working on a trail uncovered one of these pipes
and sent for me to look at it.  One thinks of wood as im-
permanent, but this log, about twelve inches in diameter
and I suppose thirty feet long, appeared to be about as
sound as a newly felled tree.  There was a little decay
at the joint but the main body of the log was good,
sound timber.

Dr. Goode built his home amid the grove where the
eighteenth green of the Homestead course is now located.
It was still there in 1891 and the site was chosen by my
father for the house he intended to build.  After Goode's
structure was torn down the rapidly developing golf
course made it evident that no dwelling should be

erected at that point. However, Goode's cellar was never filled in and the eighteenth green covers a considerable portion of it. That should make it easy to get perfect drainage and perhaps it does for, in spite of being shaded by oaks on three sides, a condition usually fatal for a green, it has always been one of the easiest to maintain.

Dr. Goode died in 1858 and the "Open Trail" up by the gardens makes a zig and a zag passing the Presbyterian Church so that the pounding of horses' feet will not disturb the slumbers of the old doctor and two of his daughters.

Apparently with the death of Dr. Goode the development of Hot Springs came to a halt. Lack of means of access by railroad, while so many other localities were thus being brought into contact with the world in general, and the fact that no commanding personality came to the Valley left it a backwater. Until that time it had been like a fertile field, which, when cleared of the original forest, receives and stimulates the seeds of cultivated plants as if through the ages it had been waiting for them. In the Valley the seeds were the advent of civilized men. However, this first urge is soon spent and then there must be cultivation for further production. The pristine stimulus was past and a new element had to come in before the Valley could move farther along the road of civilization.

1858 until 1891 was, in effect, a period of hibernation. The hotels at the Warm, the Hot and Healing passed through various hands, mostly of absentee owners. During the Civil War the hotel at Healing Springs was used as a hospital and troops marched to and fro through the Valley. No substantial construction occurred and records of events are few and far between. Gradually the hotels were drifting toward oblivion, as happened in innumerable places throughout the Virginia Alleghanies.

The story of the modern Homestead and its repercussion on the Valley begins with the acquisition of the properties at Hot Springs, on a commissioner's sale, by Colonel J. A. August and W. S. Edmond, about 1890. Shortly after their purchase they sold to those who became the present owners.

# 3. The Warm Springs

COMING to the Valley from the north or east the first of life along the Road is met at Warm Springs. Here settlers came and in the course of time the "Warm," as it is always called, flourished and had its heyday. For a long time it eclipsed the "Hot," five miles to the south, but the climax came in the middle of the nineteenth century, after which its stream of life diminished until it became, as it is today, little more than a tradition. When the Hot reached maturity the Warm was in its dotage.

The Warm never felt the advent of the machine age and such things as modern plumbing, electric light, telephones, or heating, other than by open fires, were unknown in the hotel even to the end. It had its glory, however, as one of the flowers of our civilization when there were slaves and the railways were still supplemental means of transportation. In the early nineties, a faded lady of the old regime with an aura of tradition and romance, it was shabby and down at heel.

Diligent search has failed to discover records indicating when the hotel which was standing in 1891 was built. It was apparently the second substantial hostelry there. About fifty yards south of the hotel was the Colonnade, three stories high and with a narrow terrace in front from which huge columns rose sheer to a projection of the roof. According to tradition this was erected within a few years of 1811. In 1891 there were no public rooms in the Colonnade, only sleeping quarters, but it is probable that the original construction made provision for these and they were eliminated when the main hotel was built.

It was certainly no more than a few years after the Colonnade was finished that the hotel proper was completed, a building of no architectural distinction, simple but generally pleasing to the eye. It was of three stories, in the shape of an "E" with the center projection left off. Between the ells was a porch about fifteen feet above the ground level. The southern ell, at the porch level, was a good classical Virginia ballroom, with balcony for the musicians and ceiling two stories in height. The northern ell housed the kitchen and dining room. There was only one bath tub in the building and two large public toilets. In spite of these limited facilities

well authenticated records show that, using the Colonnade
the cottages and the hotel, often as many as three
hundred people were staying at the Warm during the
summer. The construction of the hotel, Colonnade and
some of the cottages of soft local brick laid in lime mortar
was the reason for their final dissolution. What the
original roof on the hotel may have been is not known but
at some time it was replaced by a tin one. Repairs were
made from time to time but leaks occasionally developed
and when water trickled down the walls not protected
by paint, plaster and brick began to disintegrate. When
the idea of modernizing the building was finally considered
it was found the walls were so weakened they could not
carry the burden of alterations. The building eventually
became a hazard and was torn down completely in 1925.
It is interesting to note the impermanency of these early
brick buildings in the Virginia mountains. Of the many
once standing only one remains today, that at Old Sweet
Springs, which has been bought by the State and converted into an old folks' home. The Old White, at White
Sulphur, had to be razed for the same reason as was the
Warm.

There is a most delightful account of the early days
of Warm Springs, published in 1835 by a writer who used
the nom de plume of Peregrine Prolix. His description
is picturesque. Peregrine was first housed in a log cabin
much to his disgust, not mitigated when Fry, the proprietor, told him that Thomas Jefferson had spent three
weeks in the same cabin on the occasion of his last visit
to the Warm. He states that in a few days he was moved
to comfortable quarters in the main hotel, which indicates
that customs of visitors and reservation clerks have not
greatly changed in more than a hundred years.

There did not seem to be much to do except bathe in the waters, and one of the most amusing bits of Peregrine's account is that of the manner of bathing.

"The water is five feet deep for the gentlemen and four for the ladies. The two sexes bathe alternately; spaces of two hours each being allotted, from 6 A. M. to 10 P. M. You may take three baths a day without injury. To bathe comfortably you should have a large cotton morning gown of a cashmere shawl pattern lined with crimson, a fancy Greek cap, Turkish slippers, and a pair of loose pantaloons; a garb that will not consume much time in doffing and donning. Stay in the bath fifteen minutes, using very little exercise whilst in the water. As soon as you come out, hurry to your cabin, wrap yourself in a dry night gown, go to bed, cover up warm, go to sleep, get into a fine perspiration, grow cool by degrees, wake up in half an hour, dress and go to dinner with what appetite you have.

"This process, except the dinner, may be repeated twice a day with great profit and pleasure, and on one occasion, breakfast or supper can take the place of dinner. At this comfortable, well-kept and agreeable establishment, the charge is eight dollars per week, or one and half per diem; and half price for servants and horses. If you want fire in your room you have it for asking, and, in truth, every effort is used to give comfort and satisfaction to the visitors."

It is obvious that beach pajamas, usually considered an invention of the Florida East Coast in the twentieth century, were in use in the Virginia mountains almost a century before!

Prolix writes that one can take as many as three baths a day with benefit but warns against staying in the pools longer than fifteen minutes at a time. Today people often ask how long they should stay in and it is interesting to note that this fifteen minutes is still the conventional duration of a bath. A doctor of Philadelphia who visited the Warm in 1833 wrote a series of letters under the pseudonym of "Dr. O." He advised that it is dangerous to remain in longer and cites a report that Thomas Jefferson on one of the last of his many visits stayed in the baths for two hours and was afterwards of the opinion this so damaged his health that he never thoroughly recovered. Dr. O.'s attributing this remark to Jefferson is correct for we find it in a letter from Jefferson, dated December 18, 1825, to a friend.

Dr. O. had quite an adventurous trip all around. He came by stage and his account of the descent of Warm Springs Mountain is worth recording:

"Just before reaching the Warm Springs you cross a mountain called after them, of one thousand feet or more elevation; the ascent is tedious and protracted but the descent is not open to any such imputation and is indeed rather discomposing to a plain citizen's nerves, from the rapidity with which it is negotiated by the stage. Backing the horses so as to moderate the speed downwards is out of the question, for the lock on the hind wheels being once fixed on the top of the mountain, away you go like a sled upon the side of an icy hill, with short turns alternately right and left, till you get to the bottom. This manoeuvre, for such it may be called, is executed in a few minutes to the no small discomfiture of persons who have never participated in it before. It would be well before it is begun to have some understanding with the driver about speed, but when the latter is once established near the top of the mountain, the stage, from a mere vehicle, becomes a species of projectile against which the physical opposition of the wheel horses is good for nothing. To hold

on to your seat is therefore the only rule. The comfort
of this rapid descent is not at all improved by seeing
precipices of some hundred feet on one side within a short
distance of the wheel and the conviction that the whole
machinery must work perfectly true to save one from
disaster.

"The driver we had never seemed to have studied the
doctrine of centrifugal forces, and as he made one of his
left-hand turns with uncommon activity, I almost conceived that I could feel the pitch of the stage over towards
the precipice at its side. Having escaped this, I told him
that I had never seen a more unphilosophical turn than
that; though the meaning was perhaps not understood by
him, it put the passengers into a laugh, which answered
the purpose and eased them of some of their anxiety."

While both Peregrine Prolix and Dr. O. speak of
John Fry as being the proprietor of the Warm Springs
Hotel at the time of their visits, which must have been in
the early eighteen-thirties, there is some confusion on this
point.  It appears from the records that John Brockenbrough was the owner of the Warm from 1828 until 1852.
On the face of things this makes it appear that Fry and
Brockenbrough were both in command at the same time
but the probabilities are that Brockenbrough acquired
the properties from Cuthbert Bullitt's estate and that
for a time Fry (a son-in-law of Cuthbert Bullitt) remained
on, managing the hotel.

We have quite an account of Brockenbrough in the
1851 edition of Burke's "Springs of Virginia":

"Dr. Brockenbrough, the proprietor, one of the best
specimens of the 'gentlemen of the old school,' and his
venerable and elegant lady, reside at the Springs and,
with their beautiful and fascinating granddaughters, give
tone and charm to the delightful association."  Of one of

these young ladies Burke says: "Were I a poet, I would endeavour to portray the oldest of these lovely beings, as she descends the mountain of a bright summer morning, seated on her panting thoroughbred palfrey, after a long and rapid ride, her hair flowing down her shoulders and bedewed with liquid gems that fall from trees as she passes underneath their foliage . . ."

Burke is even more turgid in describing the younger granddaughter, bursting into rhyme and comparing her to Mrs. Siddons in the character of "The Tragic Muse." Calling these young ladies Brockenbrough's granddaughters was an error, but a natural one. They were really the Misses Ella and Emily Chapman, who spent much time at the Warm. On Brockenbrough's death he left a considerable fortune, including fifty-seven slaves, and in his will mentions these young ladies both as nieces and wards. One of them married a member of the Spanish Embassy to this country, named Deporstead, and the other a Prince Pigniotelli. The latter was probably of the Pignatella family, and the peculiar spelling Brockenbrough's.

Although the Warm had seen many famous visitors before Brockenbrough's day, apparently its rise to social preeminence dates from his regime. Brockenbrough leaves two monuments. During his ownership the "ladies' bath" was built. (There had been only one before, which thereafter was called the "gentlemen's bath.") It stands today just as it was then, with the invalid chair, which can be lowered into the pool, still operable. Probably every timber in both baths has been renewed in the course of over a century's exposure to the weather without and the steam from the pools within, but the structures have not been changed other than to put a new board in where one gave way.

The other standing memorial to Brockenbrough is the lovely little Episcopal Church just west of the baths. Title to the land on which this church stands is one of those things which brings gray hairs to conveyancers. When Brockenbrough finally sold the Warm Springs property he reserved the lot for the church "so long as services shall be conducted in the building," otherwise title was to revert to the heirs of the conveyor. For years now this church has had no pastor but the condition has been met by a few of the old parishioners holding one service a year. In the meantime the heirs of John Brockenbrough have scattered to the four winds. The building is well worth preserving and should be repaired before it falls down but no one will do that without title to the land and that cannot be obtained.

Most of the old registers of the Warm Springs hotel from the 1820's until it was finally closed are in the archives of The Homestead. These make interesting reading. A hotel bill in those days was obviously a simple affair compared with modern forms. It was made up of a few items, lodging and meals of course, usually followed by charges for fodder and oats for horses and in many cases board for servants. The most frequent entry, however, was for whiskey and it was a rare guest indeed who did not have that necessity on his account.

On these records will be found the names of most prominent Virginians from 1820 on. Family is important in Virginia and it is amusing to look over these records with Virginia friends. You may start out to run through the pages looking for a particular name but seldom turn over more than a few leaves of the books until you have to stop while speculation is indulged in as to whether or not a particular name is that of someone who married a great-great aunt, once removed, or is, mayhap, the ancestor of some mutual friend, or a man who played a prominent part in Virginia politics or law.

Most people want to see Thomas Jefferson's records and it is noted that his charges for "whiskey" were well up to the average of other guests. Jefferson made many visits to the Warm, frequently referred to in his voluminous writings. There is an intriguing name occurring at the Warm coincident with Jefferson's visits—that is Alexander Hamilton, and until I made some investigations in the course of preparing this volume it was generally supposed that this was *the* Alexander Hamilton. What a fascinating idea it was to think of these two enemies bathing in the pools and afterwards discussing politics over mint juleps, the making of which they were both charged with! Unfortunately, this Alexander Hamilton made his visits after the date of the Burr-Hamilton duel. Thus goes an attractive tradition.

The same fate has befallen the story of a visit by Washington. This is contained in an autograph letter of Washington which is one of my most valued possessions. My wife shares my interest in the history of the Valley and by a rather complicated series of coincidences discovered there was a collection, pretty complete, of the publications of the early nineteenth century dealing with the Virginia Springs. With much trouble and at considerable expense she acquired the collection and gave it to me as a birthday present. Among other items was this Washington letter.

The letter describes in great detail a visit to the Warm Springs of Virginia. It is of particular interest as it contains much personal news and is written in a lighter and more humorous vein than I had known was possessed by Washington. Place names have changed but the description of the trip reads exactly as if the journey was to

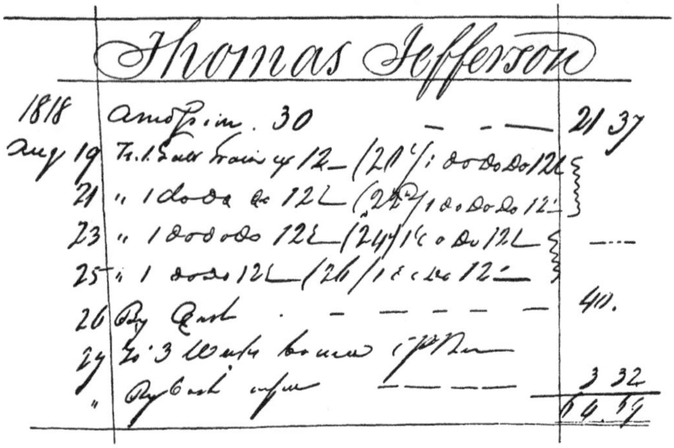

| | Thomas Jefferson | |
|---|---|---|
| 1818 | am'd brot forw. 30 — — — | 21 37 |
| Aug 19 | To 1 Gall whiskey 12— (20) 1 do do do 12 | |
| 21 | " 1 do do do 12 (22) 1 do do do 12 | |
| 23 | " 1 do do do 12 (24) 1 do do 12 | — |
| 25 | " 1 do do 12 (26) 1 do do 12 | |
| 26 | By Cash — — — — — | 40. |
| 27 | To 3 [illegible] [illegible] | |
| " | By Cash [illegible] — — — | 3 32 |
| | | 64.?9 |

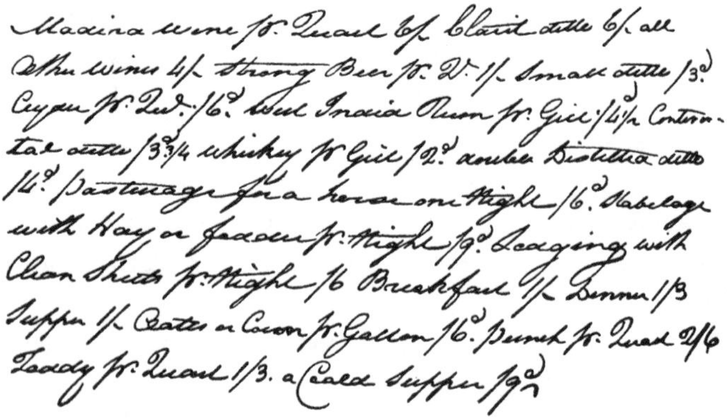

Madeira wine pr. Quart 6/. Claret ditto 6/. all other Wines 4/. Strong Beer pr. Do. 1/. Small ditto /3d. Cyder pr. Qut. /6d. West India Rum pr. Gill /4½ Continental ditto /3¾ whiskey pr Gill /2d. double Distilled ditto /4d. Pasturage for a horse one Night /6d. Stabelage with Hay or fodder pr. Night /9d. Lodging with Clean Sheets pr. Night /6 Breakfast 1/. Dinner 1/3 Supper 1/. Oats or Corn pr. Gallon /6d. Punch pr. Quart 2/6 Toddy pr. Quart 1/3. a Cold Supper /9d.

our Warm Springs. The description of the place itself, with the mountains about it, and of the mode of life, is almost perfect and just as other early writers have detailed it. Everyone accepted the letter as sure evidence that Washington had visited our Valley until a kind friend, versed in Washingtonia, presented to me irrefutable evidence that it undoubtedly was the account of a visit to what is now known as Berkeley Springs, West Virginia, then called Warm Springs.

I came to know the Warm best as an ideal objective for a horseback ride. Going up the mountain at Hot Springs, then along the top to Flag Rock and down the highway to the Warm was about nine miles, a slow ride, for only occasionally was it possible to get the horse out of a walk on the rough trail, but the views were lovely and the air bracing. With the clump, clump of the horse, coming down the steep mountain grade on the highway, you became aware of muscles normally unsuspected so that when you reached the hotel and the negro boy took your horse it needed just about the allowable fifteen minutes in the pool to limber you up. Then after the stroll back to the casino and the inevitable mint julep there was little more to be desired in the way of physical well-being. The casino, compared to the hotel and the Colonnade, was a modern affair with a wide veranda completely surrounding it. Old-timers were always sitting about, delighted to find an occasion to tell of the ancient glories of the place, and it was there that I learned the traditions and examined the old records.

In the nineties there was a brave struggle to preserve a way of life which was passing fast. Cotillions, or Germans, as they were called, were still danced occasionally during the season and it was flattering to the youth of Hot Springs when an invitation was proffered for one

of these. From the earliest days the man who could
"lead" a German was an outstanding figure and when I
danced my first, George Gibson, the last of these, held the
throne. Gibson belonged to an earlier era. He was a
brilliant and entertaining conversationalist whom we
generally found sitting on the lawn, holding forth to a bevy
of rather fragile females dressed in the frilly costumes the
Southerners liked so much. He was usually busy with a
piece of needlework, an occupation that so fascinated me
it was hard to pay attention to the talk, which was really
good. He never caught up with the mechanical age and
his adventure with a gadget at the casino bar for cutting
the ends off cigars was typical. Endeavoring to learn
how it operated he pushed a finger into the hole where the
cigar should go, losing the tip of his finger by so doing.
That was bad enough, but a few weeks later, explaining
how it had happened and showing the scar resulting, he
repeated the whole process. However, he was a wizard at
directing complicated figures on the dance floor.

By no means all followed Peregrine's advice given
in the fifties, not to remain in the pool over fifteen minutes,
and we heard stories of how it was customary to lie in the
water and have mint juleps floated out, sipping these while
lying across a rope stretched from one side of the pool to
the other. This sounds like sybaritic enjoyment and
parties are still given at the pool where the old custom is
revived. That seems to me rather a sloppy way of spoiling
a mighty good thing. A julep and a bath in the pool make
a good combination but best if taken serially; besides
some smart Alec is almost sure to make a splash and either
dilute the julep or upset it completely.

Under the usual routine no man is allowed in the
woman's pool and vice versa for the gals. Mixed bathing
was not correct when the pools were first established and

there are plenty of conservatives who insist the custom should not be changed. But for these parties only invited guests are admitted and the men's pool is used. The good Virginia ladies not only denied the men the use of joint facilities but even among themselves insisted that all should wear a bathing costume, and that is still done. These swim suits are strange contraptions, reminding one of the New England "swing clear" dresses of farm women or of pillow cases with holes cut in the corners. In the men's pool the conventional garb is that of Adam.

At one of the earliest of these mixed parties it was suggested that the manner of dressing should be reversed. The girls demurred and a compromise was reached on modern swim suits which, after all, is not much of a compromise, while the men were made to wear the women's costumes. My readers will no doubt recall Mark Twain's description in Innocents Abroad of what came back to him when his laundry became mixed up with a woman's. At all events the men appeared sufficiently bizarre and, having been allowed this much deviation from the conventional severe male garb, the men usually let fancy run and appeared in picture hats and other adornments. The girls, too, felt free to add touches here and there. A photograph of one of these parties would be worth while but someone always splashes water on the camera just as the shutter is to be clicked. When Lee Warren used to come to Hot Springs he was always eager to arrange a pool party, and in recent years Gordon Cooper and Alfred Beadleston are competently carrying on the tradition.

The last owner of the Warm before the property was purchased by the Virginia Hot Springs Company was Colonel John L. Eubank, and his place in the Virginia social hierarchy may be deduced from the fact that he was

the Secretary of the Virginia Convention which passed the
Secession Act in 1861. He was dead by the time I knew the
Warm but his wife was running the place. If in Boston
"the Cabots spoke only to the Lowells and the Lowells only
to God," at the Warm the Lees spoke with the Breckin-
ridges but Mrs. Eubank was reserved for the Deity. She
was at that time either a recluse or an invalid; after much
speculation we young Philistines could never determine
which. In any event she never came out of her cottage,
in the rear of the hotel. This cottage had a narrow porch
along the northern side with an entrance, but on the side
toward the hotel there was just one window, the sills of
which were somewhat lower than standard. There the
old lady, dressed in stiff black, could be seen sitting in her
rocking chair and to this window would come her servitors
for instruction and castigation by a bitter tongue. Some
few of the chosen guests probably at one time or another
had converse with Mrs. Eubank but that was not for the
newcomer and certainly not for sacrilegious youth from
the Hot.

There is no doubt that Mrs. Eubank not only had a
hold on her clientele but her employees worshiped her
as one who ruled by reason of a sort of Divine Right.

Horace, who now presides at the pools and can be
persuaded at times to make a mint julep as was done in
the old days, was a young boy then with two important
duties, the first, the never-ending task of filling and trim-
ming interminable kerosene lamps and the second,
trapping the skunks which at times threatened to take
possession of the place. His father was head waiter and a
finer type of old-time negro never existed. He not only
handled his job competently but, with white handle-bar
mustachios, looked the part to perfection.

For a few years after the Hot Springs Company acquired the Warm, Mrs. Eubank continued to operate it under a lease, in her own rather unconventional manner. Many of the old clientele returned but the social order which had supplied a reservoir for typical guests of the Warm was drying up. Some others, new but appreciating its charm, came and I remember particularly Otis Skinner and his daughter, Cornelia, who were there many years. After the Warm was gone she returned to the Valley, staying at Three Hills, the place Mary Johnston purchased about a mile from the Warm. I believe Mrs. Robert E. Lee spent one summer at the Warm but was a much more frequent visitor at the Hot. The following articles, copied from "The Spur" of December, 1918, concern another member of the Lee family who used to spend the summers in the Valley:

"The death of Miss Mary Custis Lee at Hot Springs, Va., in her eighty-eighth year, removes one of the most interesting links between Civil War days and the present time. And by descent she was associated also with Revolutionary days, since she was the great-granddaughter of Martha Washington. Because of this relationship, she had gathered together many buttons and other relics of George Washington. Some of the buttons were converted into medallions and were worn by her from time to time. So much interest in these relics was shown while she was at The Homestead that for a fortnight before she died she allowed them to be placed on exhibition. Miss Lee was the last survivor of the children of General Robert E. Lee and her nearest relatives are Dr. R. Bowling Lee, of New York, and R. G. Lee, of Fairfax, Va."

"Miss Lee recalled, when at The Homestead, her last visit to Warm Springs, which is only five miles away.

This was at the close of the Civil War, when she and her
sister were told that they would have to leave because the
Yankees were coming.  They had gone to the bathing
pool, which was in the same condition then as to-day,
when the Yankees actually appeared and the two women
and their mother were forced to make their escape to one
of the old hotels and thence to Millboro. Actually, the
Yankees did not enter Warm Springs until the day after
the Lees had left this old Southern resort."

The Company found Mrs. Eubank an increasingly
difficult tenant and it is doubtful if she made much of a
financial success of her lease, with changing conditions
generally and the competition of the Hot.  The Company
leased the Warm to others and then for some years tried
to operate with a manager, but it was a losing venture.
At last, in 1924, the doors to the hotel were closed forever
and it was razed in 1925.

The final burst of glory for the Warm came with the
auction just before actual demolition of the hotel, at
which everything movable was sold. Those who attended
the auction will never forget it. Of course, it drew large
numbers from Hot Springs and some from far afield and
also brought mountain people from miles around, many
of whom had never seen the Warm but to whom it was
a sort of bridge of Carcassonne. All day it went on.  A
good many things of real value were disposed of.  When
the hotel was built it was in the heart of one of the finest
forests of North America and the timber used was the
best of the wood immediately available.  The cost of
timber then was simply that of felling the trees and sawing
them into lumber and was no greater for black walnut
than for pine. Closets were not thought of in the original
design and to remedy the neglect rooms were equipped
with wardrobes or cupboards.  These were constructed

almost entirely of black walnut, with doors sawn out of clear heartwood, some of the boards thirty-six inches wide. These wardrobes were treasure-trove for cabinet-makers. When the walls of the hotel were torn down later the old beams, hand hewn and many of white oak which through the years had hardened to the texture of metal, were salvaged and now are in other buildings, starting a second century of service. Lovely old spool beds and chairs, also made of the finest woods, were disposed of. The many fireplaces were equipped with cast iron firedogs in the shape of Revolutionary soldiers. There was, of course, much junk accumulated during the last two or three generations the Warm was operated but enough remained of the good, old, pioneer craftsmanship to give a healthy respect for the skill and honesty of the early mountaineer workmen.

Some things should never have been sold, such as the four-horse coach. This specimen of colonial handiwork deserved a better fate than to form the body of a farm wagon. Many years later, in the nineteen forties, The Homestead purchased a fine example of the Brewster Coach, which shows excellent craftsmanship but for grace and lightness does not compare with the one sold at the auction.

Now there remains nothing but a few mossy foundations of the hotel. The older brick and log cabins are gone also. Some of the other cabins, built probably in the eighties, are still there, remodeled as housing for dairy employees. The spring, the pools and their bath rooms, however, are just as they have been for well over a century.

An account of the Warm would not be complete without something about Mary Johnston and her place, "Three Hills." She came to stay at the Warm just after she had written "To Have and To Hold"; royalties were no doubt large and income taxes not burdensome. Miss Johnston loved the Valley and in 1911 purchased a tract of land to the south of the Company's holdings at Warm Springs. The place was well up on the side of Warm Springs Mountain, with one of the finest views in the Valley. By 1913 she had built a lovely country house there. One of her sisters, Eloise, in whom the artistic sense took the form of love of flowers, laid out a beautiful garden with a view down Warm Springs Gap. Mary Johnston brought her whole family to live with her and it was not long before the upkeep of such an elaborate house became burdensome, particularly as she never repeated the success of "To Have and To Hold," and paying guests were taken to help meet expenses. Several cottages were erected and Eloise became the business woman of the family.

Mary Johnston lived at Three Hills until her death in 1936. She was a shy little woman, of great charm when one got to know her. She went in public very little except to swim in the Warm Springs pool, passing her days with books and writing. She was particularly fond of a walk through a tangled wilderness between her property and the Company's and built a small structure there where she could read or write. Unfortunately, when the Company dairy was moved to its present location lovelorn cows used to meander up along the fence outside the thicket and call mournfully across the hill to an eager taurus—in the end some good pasture land was fenced off to keep the bovines farther away.

Of course Mary Johnston was a product of the Old South and when the Warm was finally closed, and in fact before that, many of the die-hards of the older generation came to stay at Three Hills. Particularly during Mary's

life there were always at Three Hills people from the South
bearing great names. Both Mary and Eloise are now
dead but their sister, Elizabeth, runs the place. The
gardens are not as elaborate as they once were, and the
generation which made the life is passing, but many still
go there to enjoy the glorious sunsets down the gap, the
peace and quiet of the mountains pervading all. Only a
year or so ago, Mrs. Halsey, the wife of Admiral Halsey,
spent most of the summer there.

When it became necessary to intern the members of
the Vichy French Embassy in 1943 the State Department leased Three Hills and made a contract with the
Virginia Hot Springs, Inc., to operate it. The French
remained but a short time as the isolation seemed to
irritate them, and they were moved to the Cascades Inn.
There they remained until finally released from custody,
apparently happy enough after some peculiar rearrange-
ment of connecting rooms was worked out in what is
popularly supposed to be the French manner. Their
guarding was more or less informal, nothing like that for
the Japanese at The Homestead.

The old village of Germantown, now Warm Springs,
still has interest. Miss Somers Anderson owns a beautiful
old colonial house there, which she operates as a small inn.
Miss Anderson's mother knew more about the wild
flowers of this part of the country than anyone else. Miss
Anderson, herself, is no mean authority and has, in addition, a lovely old-fashioned garden. Miss Anderson's Inn
is a link with the old days and has many summer visitors,
such as the Daingerfields, of Kentucky, who have been
coming to the Valley literally for generations.

Another attractive house in the village is "The
Chimneys," for two decades the home of John W. Stephen-
son, one of the leading jurists of Western Virginia and a

member of the State Legislature for many years. This house is now owned by the Lee Benoists.

Some things about progress are not so good. The County has built a new courthouse of doubtful architectural character, selling the lovely old one for an inn. Then, during the excitement of the war, they changed the name of the village at Warm Springs from Germantown to Warm Springs. It had been called Germantown from the first settlers, Hessian prisoners who had come from the Shenandoah Valley, and I felt it was snobbish to discard a name given to commemorate a fine, solid strain. I don't like new names, anyway. They are now trying to change that of the colored settlement down Warm Springs Gap from the almost perfect one of Shake Rag to the banal West Warm Springs, and, up in Highland County, Crab Bottom, one of the loveliest spots in all the Alleghanies, now has its post office marked "Blue Grass." Thank goodness we still have Jerkemtight Creek.

With the passing of these old place names there is another loss. The Scotch-Irish, who made up a large percentage of the local population, brought with them idiomatic phrases and words from the home land. Out of contact with the rest of the country, these persisted but are passing with centralized schools and better communication. There is one word I have always loved. One of the earliest greenkeepers was Quigley Keyser. We had a late spring once and I asked him how the greens were. His reply was "a mite dauncey." I had never heard the word and assumed it had something to do with "dance" but found from the dictionary it was a good Elizabethan word meaning sickly. When asking for directions you are now seldom told that your destination is "a right smart piece" down the road but "crawfishy land" is still a good description of river bottom with too much gravel. Mountain honeysuckle is of course azalea. There are many curious constructions. If a dog scratches at a door you may be asked to open it for the "dog wants out" or "in" as the case may be. If you want your horse to meet you some place the groom will tell you he will "carry" your horse to wherever it may be, and he may warn you to "be a mite careful" in riding back. I have heard the expression credited to the Kentucky mountaineers of some place being "a whoop and a holler" away but here in Virginia it is a "powerful" distance. Of course, if you clear a "breshy" field you are bound to leave "stobs" to bother stock.

# 4. *I Come to the Valley*

IN THE 1880's my father, M. E. Ingalls, had by some quirk of fortune become president of the "Big Four," now one of the integers of the New York Central. He fell into this job as legal representative for some Boston capitalists. While operating the railroad he retained his connection with the men who were responsible for making the railroad executive out of the lawyer and frequently acted for them in connection with their midwestern investments. In that period railways were rapidly being merged into larger lines and, as a consequence of his familiarity with the growing network of rails in Ohio and Kentucky, my father acquired for these capitalists a small line, the Kentucky Central. This was held a short time and then sold to one of the large systems. It was a profitable operation and its success led my father to suggest to these men that C. P. Huntington, then becoming engrossed in his western activities, might be willing to sell enough of his Chesapeake and Ohio stock to give control of that road.

This undertaking was a bit too large for Boston so they went to J. P. Morgan and Company, in New York, and a syndicate under the management of that banking firm bought control from Huntington. My father was elected president of the road and operated it until the syndicate sold their holdings to the Pennsylvania in 1899.

In those days the Chesapeake and Ohio was far from the great system it has become and if its single track streaks of rust were to continue to carry trains the most active and detailed management was essential. Although learning the business from the top down, my father was the sort of man who liked the closest possible contact with anything for which he was responsible and ultimately knew every foot of track and most of the personnel.

We lived in Cincinnati, one end of the road, and as headquarters there had drawbacks it occurred to my father that he might live at almost the exact center of the line for at least part of the year and at the same time avoid the smog and heat of Cincinnati summers. He, therefore, rented "Grant's Farm," about three miles from White Sulphur. Like all who come to these mountains, my father, passionately fond of nature, fell in love with the area.

The syndicate which bought the Chesapeake and Ohio had great plans, such as steamship lines from Newport News to New England and Europe, development of new coal fields and then, fired by my father's enthusiasm, they conceived the idea of restoring to the Virginia mountains their earlier role as a vacation land. An option was taken on White Sulphur but before it could be closed one of these men, I think George T. Bliss, had an unfortunate experience with a pair of white shoes mildewing over night while visiting us at the farm with the other members of the syndicate, and vetoed any thought of putting money in a place subject to river fogs. My father then arranged for these financiers an old-fashioned driving trip around the many springs of Virginia, the result of which was the purchase of the three in the Warm Springs Valley, the Warm, the Hot, and the Healing Springs. The railroad at the same time undertook to build a branch from the main line in Covington, Virginia, to Hot Springs.

While the properties were acquired by the same group which bought the Chesapeake and Ohio, it was a venture by the individual members of the syndicate and did not involve the railroad in any way. Later on the Virginia Hot Springs Company, which was formed as the agency for the development of the properties, became indebted to the railroad for freight, materials and the like and this indebtedness was funded by bonds, but the railroad never had an equity in the property and theirs was a minority interest in the bonded indebtedness.

The original purchase by the syndicate consisted of about 4,700 acres and this has grown until it now comprises some 17,250 acres. Today the Warm Springs tract is little changed, that at Hot Springs has been rounded out, but the chief increase came from the purchase of the Rubino tract beyond Healing Springs, and an area on Warm Springs Mountain above cultivated land, extending about nine miles from Flag Rock past Bald Knob.

All the talk I heard of Hot Springs after the Valley properties were purchased meant little in my child's mind—more important was the new game I was learning. Living near Grant's Farm were a number of Englishmen and Scotchmen who had emigrated and settled in the fertile valleys. Two in particular I remember, one a red-bearded Scot from whom I heard, with wonder, a real Scotch burr. He seemed remarkable to me because he came to call astride a huge rawboned cow. Of course, a cow was not a strange animal but I had never thought of one except as a producer of milk, and was fascinated. Always asking questions, I wanted to know, "Why the cow?" "It's this way," I was told, "I like to go visiting but am apt to stay too long and neglect the farm. Now, Betsy out there, when it comes to milking time, begins to bawl and I know it's time to leave."

The other was Russell W. Montague, whose son, Carey, was just a year or so older than I. Montague had brought some golf clubs from Scotland and used to knock a ball about his pasture. Carey and I often followed and one day he took us to the farm blacksmith shop and made each of us a club. With that one to start with, I have been swinging a golf club for almost sixty years. I bear a sad reminder of that first club. Always wanting to try something new, I thought if you put the ball on a small mound of earth to hit it you ought to do still better if it were raised higher so you could swing like you would at a baseball. We set up a two-foot length of pipe, put the ball on this, and Carey took a mighty swing, which missed the ball but continued around until the club came to rest on the bridge of my nose. The outer evidence has passed away but it did something to the air passages and I am still paying for the experience.

In the early eighties my father had formed the habit of annual trips to Europe to get away from the demands of his varied interests in railways, banking and politics. These trips were interrupted for two years because he wanted to be on the ground to watch the growing pains of the railroad and Hot Springs. By 1891, however, plans for the initial development were pretty well completed, the branch railway line was pushing up the river from Covington to Hot Springs, where building was going on as fast as materials could be brought in, so the trips abroad were resumed. In 1888, he had taken my sister, Gladys, little more than a baby, and me, at the most troublesome age, along and I have a hunch he felt that this time he would get more rest if we were left at home. The Homestead was pretty well run down and the hotel at the Warm semi-fashionable, and it was decided to park us two youngsters at the Healing for the summer, where John Stimson, one of my uncles, was put in charge.

I don't remember much of this first trip to the Valley. Those were the happy days when railway presidents used their private cars as people now use motor cars and we, with Lizzie, a fine type of old-fashioned nurse, were put on the car in Cincinnati and deposited at the station in Covington. It did not make much of an impression that we should have to drive four hours after leaving the train, for we lived in the suburbs and it was forty minutes to "town" at home. We loaded into a two-seated surrey with a huge boot on the back into which the luggage was put. More often than not, heavy luggage was carried in wagons but if we had such I don't recall it. Arriving at the Healing we were ushered across the long bridge, unchanged today from what it was then, and assigned the two-story cottage at the western end, where we spent a happy summer.

There were a good many people at the Healing but I recall only a few. One man, for whom I still have a strong resentment but whose name fortunately has passed into oblivion, used to take me walking. One day we went down the highroad and then in to the last cataract of the Cascades. There were no trails along the stream but we got to the falls. Scrambling about the rocks I found the most perfect stone tomahawk I have ever seen. This man pooh-poohed my find, which I insisted on carrying home, ridiculing my prize. Finally he persuaded me to throw it away over the side of the road. When we got home I told of my find and began to regret my haste in throwing it away. The place I tossed it was by a huge sloping rock and nothing would do but Lizzie had to take me back to search for it. Many times that summer I looked in vain and not so many years ago I looked again without avail. I can only believe this man took advantage of a small boy and returned himself to salvage the treasure.

Another guest was a funny little round fat man who took a fancy to me. Any sort of shooting apparatus had fascinated me since I knew what such things were, and I owned an air rifle. One day after the mail was in this man called to me and said he had just received a Flobert rifle and, if I would like, he would show me how to shoot.

With this began a beautiful friendship. This man was Jacob Rubino, who soon thereafter purchased what was known as "The Little Healing" and built as his residence what is now the Cascades Club. Jakey later became involved in a complicated lawsuit with the Hot Springs Company but I never lost the affection formed for him in the walks we took, I proudly carrying the little rifle and shooting under his careful tutelage at any and everything. Jakey had an eventful life of ups and downs but when the final accounts are cast up I hope he gets a great big credit for the happiness he gave a small boy.

M. E. Ingalls never held office in the Hot Springs Company, the corporation through which the syndicate held their properties in the Valley, but from 1891 until 1914 nothing was ever done without his approval and very little except under his direction. Decatur Axtell, an engineer and later a vice president of the Chesapeake and Ohio, was made president, a position he filled for many years. He was a little over six feet tall, pompous and almost cadaverous, with a strange, husky voice. I came to know him better in the course of time and, while he always took on the character of a lay figure, learned that he had human qualities. This discovery was made on one of the earliest occasions I went into the Homestead Bar. I saw Axtell, full of dignity, walk in, nod to the barkeeper and stand before the bar. One, and then a second, over-size pony of bourbon whiskey was put before him and downed with silent efficiency. Then, just as majestically, he walked out.

Axtell knew little about a hotel or the manifold problems of a resort but was a capable engineer and the immense amount of construction, really the building of the modern Homestead, which continued during the long years of his presidency was done soundly and well. Axtell made a fine choice in the engineer he obtained for direct supervision, in the person of C. W. Richardson. The immense network of piping for water supply was put in by Richardson and, although greatly extended and enlarged, the principal mains he installed are still operating efficiently after more than half a century.

Richardson was a man who believed in building honestly and permanently. One of my first encounters with him was about planting some trees. Wanting a quick effect, I suggested maples. "But maples won't be good for more than sixty years," he said, "we want these to be here when we are gone and oaks should be used." Oaks were put in.

Fortunately, we still have a Richardson. His son, Bruce, although never a regular employee of the Company was also an engineer and for years was employed for special problems. The very beautiful map of company property hanging by the porter's desk is his work and he drew the map shown in the front and back of this book. Bruce, Jr., is with us now and most visitors to The Homestead feel his greeting is one of the things that makes a return so pleasant.

Among other things, the elder Richardson built the present highway from Hot Springs to Warm Springs. The old Jackson River Turnpike had served the Valley and the stock of this, with other assets, was acquired by the Hot Springs Company. This turnpike followed the route of the present back road from just behind the eighth tee of the Homestead Course, up and down hill to Warm Springs. From that point to The Homestead traces of the old road can still be seen crossing the eighth fairway and again just below the second green, and down below the eighteenth green where it crossed the creek about where the bridge used by horses and carriages going to and from the stable is now located. It then went past the front door of the old Homestead, down the Valley and over the mountain to Covington. A new location giving access to the railway station was required and when the boulevard, as it was called, was built the connection for the old turnpike to the new road was made by the eighth green and the turnpike across the golf course abandoned. For many years the Company continued to collect tolls both on the boulevard, which followed a private right-of-way, and on the turnpike. The house by the eighth hole was built for a toll house. With the coming of automobiles the turnpike accumulated a huge deficit in operating cost and an even larger surplus of ill will through collecting tolls, so in the early twenties the Turnpike Company and the boulevard were graciously presented to the State.

## 5. *The Ingalls Family Follows the Road*

IN 1892 my eldest sister was seriously ill and to get her out of the Cincinnati heat my father built his first house at Hot Springs.

Before moving my sister, the rest of the family went ahead to get settled. Rails had already reached Hot Springs but for some reason we went by train to Millboro and from there by stage. Loaded into three-seated surreys we wound down the hill to Millboro Springs, then but a ghost of an early spa, up along the Cowpasture to a stop at Windy Cove Church. I believe this was the first time my father had taken that drive and I doubt if he knew much of the church or its history. Probably he stopped, struck with its simple, dignified architecture and lovely setting in a grove of trees, or perhaps at the instigation of a talkative driver looking for a chance to blow his horses. We walked around and into the church and examined the graves behind it. The church was then, as now, of interest in itself and as one of the landmarks in the settlement of Bath County, marking the first effort of those who came from the Shenandoah Valley through the break in the western mountain wall of this Valley called Buffalo Gap to found a permanent community. I may have heard some of the history of Windy Cove Church on that trip but most of it has been picked up piecemeal from time to time in later years.

Windy Cove got its name from the cave in the limestone hill just north of the church, out of which a current of air always flows, warm in winter and cold in summer. This cave has another opening at a higher elevation some distance away on the McLaughlin farm, which probably accounts for the circulation of air. By the entrance to the cave, in my early recollections, were two crude drawings of horses; one was apparently well authenticated as the work of Indians, the other more or less modern. These, as well as the original opening of the cave, are now lost, having been eliminated when this limestone hill was used as the quarry to supply stone at the time Route 39 was hard-surfaced. There is an ugly scar where the quarry is still worked, but after passing that, a beautiful stretch of placid river beside the road down to the church lot.

One of my pleasantest memories is going down this road, on a shooting trip, and seeing a deer, roused by hunters, stop on the opposite bank, listen, then plunge into the river and swim across. I have never had a desire to shoot a deer and just stopped to watch the swim; a shake and look behind and then he bounded away over the road and up the bank on my side of the river.

The settlers in this section, as distinguished from simple adventurers, were mostly of good Scotch-Irish stock. Later, after the Revolutionary War, there were added many "Dutch," that is descendants of the Hessian prisoners of war, who drifted up through the Cumberland valley of Pennsylvania into the Shenandoah and thence to the headwaters of the James. They were practical men, looking for good farms, and rapidly spread up and down the Cowpasture, a name they substituted for the more musical Indian one of Wallawhatoola, and its tributary, the Bullpasture, It was some time before they reached the Warm Springs Valley and the headwaters of the other branch of the James, as they were checked by the barrier of the Warm Springs Mountain. The same barrier blocked the railway, which to get to Hot Springs from Millboro, an air line of about fifteen miles, makes a sixty-mile loop to the south.

The leaders of these settlers was Colonel Meriwether Lewis, who established his farm, on which a fort was built, upstream on the Cowpasture about eight miles from Windy Cove. Other settlements were made and farms established at Windy Cove (Fort Dickinson), Nimrod Hall and Wallawhatoola, about three miles south of Windy Cove.

These hardheaded Scotch-Irish were an independent lot. For quite a while none of them bothered about such things as legal title to their farms and it was not until 1750, only one year before the Lewises got their patent at Warm Springs, that the first grant was made along the Cowpasture to Adam Dickinson. The settlers were independent people in other ways and among them were Presbyterians, though the Commonwealth of Virginia only recognized the Church of England. They wanted their preaching but their heterodoxy was to make trouble for them.

There is a confusion of names which makes the very earliest beginnings of the Windy Cove Church somewhat uncertain. It is claimed there was preaching in 1747 and probably earlier, by one John Craig. It seems strange that, by reliable records, in 1749, John Craighead, a minister who had been regularly ordained in Scotland, acquired for himself a home on the Sitlington farm, down the river from Windy Cove. On this property the first Windy Cove Church was built. Craighead was unquestionably an historic character but the similarity of names suggests to the critical investigator that the name Craig is not authentic.

This first church was a log structure with a fireplace at one end and was equipped with racks for rifles and portholes from which these might be fired. There is a tradition, for which I can find no confirmation in the church records (which are continuous from 1749), that the congregation was once at worship when word came that an Indian raid was in progress.

Certain it is that after Braddock's defeat in 1755 and until the Battle of Point Pleasant the Indians were a menace to settlers. Ultimately they burned this first church and murdered, raped and made slaves of those living at Windy Cove, the Venable farm and Green Valley, a few miles to the east. During those years the Cowpasture River valley was not the peaceful, quiet farming country it has become.

The atmosphere of pioneer Virginia became uncongenial to Reverend Craighead and around 1760 he moved to Mecklenburg County, North Carolina, taking with him a number of families who had settled in the Windy Cove district. Craighead was one of the moving spirits in drawing up the Mecklenburg Declaration in 1774, the first claim for the independence of the Colonies.

The motives behind the hegira of Craighead and his flock were undoubtedly mixed. We run into the old question as to whether the American Colonists faced the frontier in a search for freedom and independence or to better their economic condition. Those who would ascribe the first motive say the trouble was the intolerance of Virginia's religious laws. Until 1785, when Jefferson obtained from the Assembly his famous statute assuring religious freedom, only regularly ordained pastors of the Anglican Church had the rights of and could perform the duties of ministers of the gospel. Craighead was a Presbyterian, so if any of his flock wanted to be married with benefit of clergy it was necessary for them to make the long trek to Staunton. While other denominations were not restrained from holding services, these were clearly extra-legal and no formal church organization could be formed.

On the other hand, the atmosphere of the Cowpasture was not conducive to material prosperity. Frequent Indian raids made life uncertain, and there was no organized government, for not until 1750 was there even the beginning of settled land titles. The rugged nature of the terrain, except for fertile river bottoms, severe winters, and the probability that the best land had been taken up by such hardy pioneers as the Lewises undoubtedly discouraged many who had come looking for a land flowing with milk and honey. As with all new developments, rosy dreams were held out to prospective settlers. A pamphlet covering a somewhat later period extols the fertility of the Deeds Country near Bath Alum as an earthly paradise where the griefs of the farmer would be eliminated, and many no doubt came with similar expectations. In this Deeds Country of thousands of acres, only the Plecker and Stanley farms were ever established.

At all events the Windy Cove Church languished until 1766 when another church was erected on the limestone hill to the north of the present building. This, too, was a log structure with portholes and rifle racks. The country was becoming more settled and in a few years this was inadequate and a third church was built on the site of the present one. This served until 1838 when the building now to be seen was erected. This was still a frontier structure, the bricks burned there beside the river, nails hammered out and timbers sawn on the site.

We have the roster of the congregation in 1838, consisting of seventy-nine names, and it is interesting to note that all but a small percentage are those of families still prominent in the affairs of Bath County.

It is probable that no architect was employed when the church was built and that may well account for its good lines. These pioneers were craftsmen, concerned with functional design only, and they built honestly and simply. The church and graveyard, seventeen miles from Hot Springs, are well worth a visit.

So, over the covered bridge beyond Windy Cove we went, feeling a bit eerie as we drove past Bath Alum, built just after the Civil War but then deserted—haunted, I was told, by the ghosts of those who had died in an epidemic presumably, in the light of today's knowledge, because the highly charged mineral spring from which the place was named was contaminated by surface drainage. When the Chesapeake and Ohio Railway was pushed beyond Staunton there was no longer the train of travelers going by highway to the Warm, the Hot, the Old Sweet or White Sulphur, and the potential business for Bath Alum disappeared. It was at that time a lovely brick building, with one of its most interesting features the magnificent hand-hewn timbers used in its construction. The bricks too were handmade and weathered to a lovely color. The hotel was not large, probably accommodating, even with a number of cottages, only around seventy-five guests. Shortly after we came to Hot Springs it was bought by Dr. Henry S. Pole, a physician at Hot Springs, who for a short time operated it as a hotel. It was a favorite picnic ground and luncheon place for the young people from Hot Springs, riding and driving over the mountain.

Bath Alum is almost a thousand feet lower than Hot Springs and, sheltered by mountains, the summer climate was not attractive enough to enable its reestablishment as a resort. After changing hands a number of times Bath Alum was purchased by Mr. C. M. Hester, of Washington, who has razed the old buildings and developed a very handsome country place, with the dwelling house on the site of the old hotel.

One thing still glorious there is the rhododendron growing to the east of the highway from Bath Alum to the Mare's Run Ford, a distance of about a mile.

When we came to that ford, where the four-mile pull begins to the pass across the Warm Springs Mountain, my father insisted that the active members of the party get out and walk to save the horses. I suspected that it was really the walk he was interested in and felt it was a long, dusty trudge.

Time plays tricks on memory, and I don't know whether it was on this first trip that I saw the teams outspanned by the ford or whether on one of the many later ones. These transport wagons were like nothing I have ever seen elsewhere, not the old-fashioned covered wagons of the western country but simply overgrown farm wagons with rectangular beds, drawn by four horses. They carried such bulky items as flour and the like, piled to the top of the sideboards, and for protection against the weather usually had a tarpaulin stretched over the load. Everything about the wagons, wheels, axles, and all was of massive construction. In addition to the conventional brakes they all carried sprags which could be slipped under the wheels, and at times you would see them coming down steep hills dragging, in addition, a log behind them.

In the trip to Highland and Pocahontas Counties the ford at Mare's Run was usually made an overnight stop, and sometimes as many as ten of these wagons would be outspanned at that point. It was a weird sight and one which gave a thrill to the beholder. Naturally, the drivers were rough, independent men, dressed for all weather and with not much opportunity for shaving or bathing. There was always a fire going and some little cooking, and the horses tethered to trees, wagons standing around and the men gathered about the fire made quite an impressive picture. The regular schedule was to arrive in the late afternoon and pick up and move in the early morning hours, well before daybreak, to get the long pull up the Warm Springs Mountain over before the heat of the day.

Not till many years after the railroad was extended to Hot Springs did the Chesapeake and Ohio build a line up the Greenbrier, and well on into the twentieth century all supplies for Marlinton, the county seat of Pocahontas County, West Virginia, and Monterey, the county seat of Highland County, Virginia, were hauled in these wagons. For the matter of that, there is no railway today to Monterey and it is only within the last few years that a paved highway has run there. Monterey is about the same distance from rail at Hot Springs and at Staunton but its supplies and produce now roll on rubber.

It was largely because Highland County had to produce what it could get to market by its own power that grazing developed as it did. Today, the rolling uplands of that county furnish some of the finest bluegrass pasture in the country; looking at the fields full of fat beef cattle, it is hard to realize there can be a shortage. It is a lovely drive to Highland from Hot Springs, with beautiful high scenery.

The road up the Warm Springs Mountain, rising from about thirteen hundred feet elevation to twenty-nine hundred, was a long, hot and dusty one. Crooked as it seems to the high speed motorist of today, it is a super-highway compared to what the early travelers had to use. You can still see traces of the old road, which went straight up the hollow, culminating at the pass. Also, if you look carefully you can see the old trenches and breastworks thrown up by Union or Confederate troops to block the highway, one of the gateways into the Shenandoah Valley from the Southwest. Looking at the steepness of the old road and the rugged terrain on each side, one wonders why it was ever thought necessary to add artificial barriers to hold back a hostile force.

ML

# 6. Hot Springs in the Early Nineties

AT THE TIME the property was acquired by the syndicate The Homestead was a typical southern resort hotel, resting comfortably along the ridge overlooking the casino lawn. It was built of wood throughout, with hand-hewn timbers of oak, pine and walnut and clapboarding of fat pine, the tall columns of the east porch lending dignity to the structure. It had no plumbing other than a few public toilets, it was heated by open fires and lighted by oil lamps. About the grounds were a number of cabins or cottages, rather crude affairs. There was also a foursquare, three-story brick building west of the main hotel, which had some large rooms considered most desirable and often occupied by people who wanted to be out of the hotel itself, though this annex was mostly used as bachelor quarters.

In addition to the hotel there were the mineral springs, natural phenomena useful for medical purposes. Experience of more than a century with these waters had developed a technique and a certain amount of equipment for their use. Shelters were built over some of the springs reputed to have curative properties when used internally. However, drinking the waters had never been stressed and was but a side issue, a concession to fashion at other spas. The main asset was the use of the waters for bathing. They had one advantage over almost every mineral spring theretofore known in that they flowed from the ground at temperatures which admitted of their use without cooling or heating. There has always been a question as to whether or not the beneficial use of thermal waters is lost with a change of temperature; it is certain that even a short exposure to the atmosphere and either the addition or subtraction of heat will change their characteristics.

These springs come out of the ground in a small area not over a few hundred feet in any dimension, yet, strangely enough, they all are different in temperature, quantity of flow and chemical content. This is all the more strange as where the water flows from the ground there cannot be found any well-defined channel through which it is led to the surface from the depths out of which it has come. Over the course of time, however, different orifices had been isolated, some within a few feet of each other, and from these openings the waters were led in wooden pipes, such as those Dr. Goode had installed for his sanitary water supply, to sundry edifices for bathing purposes. These bathhouses were in about the location of the bowling green next to the casino. The principal building was the "Pleasure Pool," enclosed in a rectangular building probably about one hundred feet long and twenty-five feet wide. A partition in the center made, in effect, two pools, one for men and the other for women, and the waters were a general mixture from all the springs. The largest of the springs and the one with the boldest and hottest flow was called the "Boiler Spring."

In addition to the Pleasure Pool there were two smaller buildings to which the waters of one particular spring were led. This was the "Spout Spring" and it was on the treatments given with its waters that the reputation of Hot Springs as a spa was founded. The baths, one for men and one for women, were so arranged that the water was introduced by a spout or nozzle somewhat more than shoulder high, with the force generated by the fall of approximately ten feet from the spring to the spout opening. The bather stood or, if an invalid, sat on a wooden chair, and allowed the stream from the spout to play on various portions of the anatomy—this constituted the famous "Spout Bath." When it was first designed and used, no one knows. Dr. Goode widely advertised it but there is no reason to suppose that such use was his invention for if it had been the probabilities are he would have boasted of that fact. It is a pretty good bet that the invalids visiting Bullitt in the eighteenth century were pummeled by such a stream of water.

There was another bathhouse called the "Plunge." This housed the octagonal spring in front of the present bathhouse, which is as it was then except that the structure covering it is gone. Its flow is now used for the swimming pool in the bathhouse. The temperature of this spring is lower than the hot springs used for treatments and is about eighty-six degrees.

M. E. Ingalls, who from first to last was the driving power in the development of the Valley properties, had a deep personal interest in spas. His father had been miserable toward the end of a long life, from rheumatism, and he himself had battled with that or gout off and on. He had taken the "cure" at various European spas and had become thoroughly convinced that such a regime was of immense benefit for the busy man, particularly when the bloom of youth was gone. It seemed logical that the aim should be to make Hot Springs a true spa.

The first step toward modernization was taken as soon as materials could be brought to Hot Springs by rail and the Virginia Hotel was built. This had steam heat and plumbing and some very attractive rooms, but it did not take long to recognize that its location was a mistake. There is an explanation if not an excuse for this. Many of the finest hotels in Europe were "station" hotels and it seemed a splendid idea to have the new hotel and the railway station under the same roof. The fact that locomotives belching soft coal smoke under windows might be a detriment, that placed at the lowest point of the valley there would be no view from the windows, and that because of the terrain there could not be adequate grounds were discoveries made shortly after it was completed.

For a few years after 1892 the "swank" accommodations at Hot Springs were in the Virginia. As the work of equipping the old Homestead with modern conveniences progressed more and more people preferred it, but the Virginia lasted somewhat longer as the favorite because when it was opened a new element came into the life of Hot Springs through the discovery of two glorious seasons in this climate. Up to that time no one thought of the Virginia mountains except as a place to go for the summer months, but now, with a comfortable all-weather hotel, spring and fall came into their own. Until restorations had gone far enough so The Homestead was also comfortable when the days got cold, people perforce stayed in the Virginia, but its popularity waned fast. After a few years it became what it is now, a dormitory for the upper range of employees, with offices for doctors and the like on the lower floors. It had a brief period of glory when The Homestead burned in 1901 and was again filled with guests during the rebuilding.

The next move after the completion of the Virginia was to have a building for the baths. The firm of Yarnall and Goforth were retained as architects and before the first plans were drawn they made a trip to Europe for the study of sundry Kurhausen there. Of the various European spas Aix-les-Bains had waters most similar to those at Hot Springs. It is probable that Dr. Goode's methods of using the mineral waters may have been copied from Aix, for we find in one of the editions of Moorman's Springs of Virginia, published in the middle of the nineteenth century, that the two places were compared and many similarities noted.

By 1892 the bathhouse was completed and in operation. In designing the bathhouse the central purpose of developing but not changing the method of using the springs was kept in mind. This consisted basically of two processes, first soaking in hot water and then applying the spout. Naturally the bathhouse has had extensive study since its first construction. Many refinements have been added. It has serious defects, such as the rather peculiar and awkward arrangement of floor levels, but it is a credit to the architects that nothing better than the original design has been found in spite of the miles traveled and the thousands spent on investigation.

By the end of 1893 the foundations for the ultimate development of The Homestead were pretty complete. The annual report issued by the corporation in that year tells in the way of figures what had been done. As an example of the way in which the value of the dollar has melted since that time these have interest. It was reported that the cost of the Virginia was $112,000, that of the bathhouse $154,000 and of ten "modern" cottages, completely furnished, $17,000. This last figure is particularly significant. Naturally the cottages as they now stand are quite different but, according to the standards of the times, they were comfortable and modern when first constructed. Yet the entire cost of the ten would not duplicate two of the present cottages; in fact, little would be left after paying for one if furnishings were included.

# 7. *The Modern Homestead Comes into Being*

D URING the first few years after the syndicate acquired their holdings in the Valley construction demanded all attention and management was a secondary consideration. In 1894, Fred Sterry was brought in as manager of The Homestead, a position he held until 1914. Sterry came from a hotel in Lakewood, New Jersey; later on he took over the Poinciana and subsequently, as manager of the Plaza in New York, became one of America's most prominent hotel executives. Whether he would stand comparison with some of the present-day hotel executives, highly trained for a most technical industry, may be questioned but it is certainly true that during his regime the basic principles under which The Homestead has since been conducted were determined and the character of its guests established. There are many still coming to The Homestead who made their first visit during his time.

When Sterry came the remodeling of the old Homestead was about completed, covering almost the same ground as the main section of the present building. When it was rebuilt after the fire of 1901 the ground floor plan was substantially the same as that for the old building and the main feature, the lobby, was copied almost exactly by Elzner and Anderson, the architects. Incidentally, even today, but more so in earlier times, I have to correct visitors who would ascribe its design to Stanford White; I suppose this is a compliment to the splendid proportions of the room but White never had anything to do with it. Floor levels were different, in accordance with the conventional idea of southern building that the first important floor should be well above the ground. Most of the old hotels, like that at the Warm, had their offices and public rooms a story above the ground and The Homestead followed this pattern. I have a suspicion that termites are not as new as we are led to believe, for through the Carolinas and Georgia many of the semi-great wooden plantation houses stand on eight and ten foot pillars of brick, to avoid contact of timbers with the soil.

A wide staircase ran from a porte cochere in front of the old building to the office in the lobby. The ground floor was filled with accounting offices, barber shop,

billiard room and bar. This latter was an attractive
affair with magnificent mahogany counter and shiny
brass rail. It was presided over by Jimmy Long, for
many years a character at Hot Springs. In the bar
Jimmy wore the usual white apron but when off duty
he clothed his small body in a severely cut morning coat
and pin-striped trousers and, carrying a gold-headed
cane, strolled about the golf course with the dignity of a
Presbyterian minister, which he resembled.

The old bar was strictly taboo for the youngsters
but I recall it as an intriguing place and Choteau Walsh,
Carl Brandt and I used to sneak into the adjoining
billiard room to play, until sooner or later one of us would
gash the cloth on a table and be chased away by Jimmy
and kept out until we made our peace.

The first time I ever entered the bar legally was when
some older member of the family, I think my brother,
George, had a birthday party with the celebration taking
place after the dancing. These elders usually adjourned
to the bar when the music ceased, while I had to go off to
bed. This time I was allowed to be present. As a guest
of honor, Li Hung Chang, the Chinese elder statesman,
then Minister in Washington, was invited. A Chinese,
particularly when dressed in Mandarin robes, was a being
of another world to me and I followed him around with
what must have been bumptious curiosity. He came to
the party early and I was amazed that he behaved just
like anyone else except that he seemed to have a bottom-
less capacity for champagne. The evening wore on with
much singing and many toasts until there came a time
when Li Hung Chang arose in his gorgeous yellow and
gold robes and said he wanted to add his word of con-
gratulations on the occasion. In fairly good English
he made a graceful speech and then said, "I must tell you

how much I admire your country. Now I will sing to you your national anthem in Chinese." (This was during the Spanish-American War.) In a rather flat voice he then proceeded to sing "There'll be a Hot Time in the Old Town Tonight." That just about broke up the party. Everyone tried to learn the Chinese words, with the old gentleman waving his arms and leading the chorus. Many other parties were held in this room but I believe this one marked the all-time high.

It was in the nineties that fashionable New York and Philadelphia discovered what Hot Springs was like in October and began to come in ever-increasing numbers. I did not see much of this life for by the twenty-first of September I always had to go back to St. Mark's or Harvard. How I hated to leave! The last ten days of every summer I would take long rides and say good-bye to the mountains—and often to the girl of that year as well. I have a feeling the climate must be changing for I nearly always saw the beginning of the fall coloring, and in recent years we haven't had much color before October. Perhaps it was only because I was so anxious to see it that the occasional tupelo flamed brightly enough to let my imagination do the rest.

It was in the nineties, too, that my mother put her ineradicable mark on Hot Springs, not that she was much interested in all the building or modernization that was going on, quite the contrary. She was immensely fond of driving and I recall that when they changed the location of the highway around the Cascades Gap just below Eden Church she was terribly upset. The change eliminated two railway crossings and a rather troublesome ford but the new road left a sweet log cabin, always surrounded with flowers, high and dry and out of sight from the road. For almost a year she refused to take that drive although it was one of her favorites. Nor did she have much use for sports other than as a means of getting the menfolks out of the way and letting them work off surplus energy.

She had two passions to which she devoted unending energy, one for people and the other for flowers or any other sort of planting. Her love of people was completely catholic. She enjoyed entertaining and did it excellently but did not restrict her affections and interest to the acquaintances who came to dinner. In her drives about the country she made friends at every house and farm on the way. There were crude characters in the Valley in those days, like the mountaineer, with typical moth-eaten beard, who climbed into my father's car by the observation platform when the train stopped at Cedar Creek water station and informed me he would like to go inside as he had never seen a "winder" car before—his only experience was with construction trains. All sorts of queer characters came to the house, bringing my mother gifts from field and forest, or their troubles, which they knew she would understand and solve. One of the happiest things about living at Hot Springs is the friendly attitude of the old residents and this relationship could never have come about but for her and, later on, my sister with her visiting nurse and Community House activities.

We six children were always urged to have friends visit for a meal or a month and we took good advantage of the chance. My mother was a natural hostess and in such matters as seating the right people next to each other was almost a genius. Most of all, I think she liked her Sunday afternoon teas, where everyone was welcome and came in droves. The huge porch on Ingallston, now called Fairacre, seldom had more than limited standing room on those days.

She satisfied her love for flowers and shrubs by never-ending planting.  Taking mighty little interest in the hotel, in fact, regarding it as rather a nuisance, anything about the grounds had to have her approval.  Early she got hold of a mountaineer—I called him "Old Man Hodge" but he could not have been so old as he was only a bit over eighty when he died a few years ago.  Hodge was a potterer to the nth degree and slow beyond all patience but he shared with my mother the gift of "green fingers." I can see her yet, early in the morning, long before break-fast, walking around with trowel in hand and followed by Hodge, his inseparable wheelbarrow loaded with plants. Mother died thirty years ago and with the changes time has brought in buildings, paths and the like, most of the shrubbery and flowers she so loved are gone.  The spruce in front of the Homestead entrance and the huge silver maples along cottage row still stand as monuments to her love for putting things in the ground and making them grow.

By the end of the century many of the "furriners" who were to come to the Valley had arrived, building houses large and small, some elaborate country places and others with just a flower garden.  Very largely it was these people who set the tempo of social life which, melding in with that of The Homestead, has done so much to make Hot Springs what it is today.  In 1891, there was only one house substantial enough to be called a "country place," the one owned by the Lanier Dunns at the entrance to Dunn's Gap, with the spring which flows on through the gap rising right in the front lawn.  This house is supposed to have been built in the latter part of the eighteenth century by a man named Cowardin. On the maps his name is preserved by calling the stream Cowardin's Run and the gap Cowardin's Gap but, while the stream is frequently referred to by the official name, you might puzzle any local resident if you asked where Cowardin's Gap is but would get a ready answer if you asked for Dunn's Gap.

There is a legend that the house was originally built as a tavern; it was located on the old toll road, but I have been unable to verify this. Later on the place was owned by the famous Daingerfield family of Kentucky, many members of which still visit the Valley. In 1882, William McKee Dunn purchased the property and gave it to his son, Lanier, who then came with his family to live in the Valley. When I arrived on the scene there were three lovely daughters and a son, McKee, two of the girls near my age and McKee a few years younger. The older members of the family were important but for me the real focus was the girls. Many times I trudged over the dusty road to call, carrying my twenty-two and wreaking havoc on the chipmunks which darted out from the brambles growing up in the snake fences, bordering the highway as they do now. Once in a while I would condescend to ride over with my sister, Gladys, in the governess' cart behind the pony.

One remembers some "firsts" in life and one of mine was the day when for some reason I could not see the girls and McKee wanted to go fishing. The snobbery of a few years difference in age during the early teens (how little they count now!) made me rather miffed, but I went with McKee and caught my first trout in the pool just above the first crossing of the creek by the highway down the gap. The pool is still there and I seldom pass without stopping. I have caught untold trout since and many in dramatic circumstances and places but none will ever count as much as that one, hauled out by a string on the end of a stick.

After his father's death McKee inherited the place and when he married Mildred Eddy they remodeled it, keeping all the old charm and beautifully landscaping it.

Kipling wrote a story in which a mountaineer of India wished for vengeance but would never leave his hills to seek his enemy. When asked why, his reply was that a mountain man always returns to his hills, and ultimately that happened in the story. That is true of Hot Springs, for after going far afield Dr. Louis Cowardin came back to the land of his grandfather and for many years practiced dentistry at Hot Springs. I owe many things to Uncle Louie. He taught me to shoot quail and it was a somewhat painful lesson for my nerves. Uncle Louie shot a fine old English hammer gun and, believing in being always ready, carried it cocked over his shoulder. What I recall most of those hunts was following him through brambles, looking into the dark muzzle and hoping a twig would not snap back onto the trigger. Nothing ever happened, however, except to impress on me the supreme importance of not inflicting similar mental agony on others.

Uncle Louie tried to teach me to fish but there he failed. He wanted meat and was a bait fisherman, and I never learned the art. An art it is I know, for one day I stood with him on a rock above a pool and, fishing with identical bait and even exchanging rods from time to time, passed most of a lovely August day catching one small sunfish while he pulled from that hole fifteen bass, the largest just under three pounds. I quit then and there and afterwards wandered up and down the stream casting, getting my share of fish though he pulled in the large ones.

It was in the course of this fishing that I saw the one case of death by snake bite in my experience. One other I know of by hearsay. Uncle Louie and I had a boat on the Jackson which we kept at the railroad water tank at Cedar Creek, ten miles below Hot Springs. The water tender took care of the boat and we used to go down on a train in the morning, returning by the night one about ten o'clock. One night we brought the boat back after fishing and found the water tender dying. It had been a warm evening and he had lain down under his tank and dozed off. Waking suddenly, he felt something on his chest and put up his hand to grasp a four foot-rattler. The snake struck twice in his neck. Possibly the man might have been saved today, but a double strike in such a spot by a large rattler, even if ours are not as venomous as those farther south, is bad medicine. Many years later, on a coon hunt, my wife was bitten, but through the cuff of an old-fashioned leather automobile gauntlet and, except for a painful arm for some time, suffered no ill effect.

Although it was some years before they acquired a house in the Valley, one of the earliest and most important of the immigrant families was the Calderon Carlisles, when they first came, spending the summers in one of the "new" cottages which were built in 1892. Mr. Carlisle was a distinguished lawyer. With the simplicity of youth, I remember looking at him and wondering how he could represent Spain when we were at war with that country, as I knew him to be a man of remarkable character and ability. Later, I found he had been counsellor and legal advisor to the Spanish Legation, as he was to the British Embassy and to several other foreign missions. In those days the missions had no legal counsellors of their own attached to the Embassy or Legation staffs.

Mr. Carlisle suffered greatly from neuritis and coming to the cottage one might see him holding his arm, his face almost livid with pain, but so soon as he caught sight of a visitor all evidence of suffering vanished and he became one of the most charming of men. He was wonderfully educated and a splendid raconteur. I remember Mrs. Calderon Carlisle mostly as a game chaperon, who, with her cousin, Mrs. Wortham, could always be counted upon to meet the proprieties when we wanted to head off on a riding or driving trip. The two children, Mary and Mandeville, with my sister and myself soon became an almost inseparable foursome. Mary was, and still is for the matter of that, an accomplished musician. She could make music with any sort of instrument and was, furthermore, generous with her gift. She would play serious or jazz as occasion demanded and when she and Mandeville got together, with his lovely baritone, it made any party. Walter Bruce Howe joined our foursome before long and ultimately married Mary. She later went in seriously for composing and concertising under the name of Mary Howe.

A few years later the Carlisles purchased the cottage adjoining the Axtell house, which had been built by L. F. Sullivan, and lived there many years. Later on, when Mrs. Carlisle died, this cottage was purchased by Mrs. A. Kelly Evans and razed to improve the grounds of the Pink Cottage, which Mrs. Evans' son, "Conky" Whitehead, had bought.

A bit later than the period I am writing of Mary trained a community chorus which so long as under her guidance was most successful. Just a few years ago she came back to spend some time at Hot Springs and for a while revived choral singing, this time with the colored population. This chorus still exists but, without someone like Mrs. Howe for inspiration, has not the vigor of early days. Ruby Donaldson, wife of the head bellman, keeps it going and several times a year concerts are given in the Liberty Theatre in the village, the proceeds going to the

THE MODERN HOMESTEAD COMES INTO BEING

Visiting Nurse Association.  Perhaps the present-day concerts are a bit more sophisticated and less spontaneous but there are some appealing voices and the sincerity with which the spirituals are sung makes them well worth while.

Very early Mrs. George Gunton purchased the property at the top of Eddington's hill, the divide between Warm Springs and Hot Springs, where a modest house had been built; this she eventually developed into one of the finest places in the Valley.   While Mrs. Gunton was quite a remarkable person herself, her advent was noteworthy because she brought with her a daughter who for many years was important in the life here.   The daughter, then Mrs. English, had had an unfortunate first marriage and was a divorcee.

Mrs. Gunton was one of the first in the fight for woman's suffrage, when it took courage and a disregard for convention to go all out for woman's rights.   She had gotten rid of one husband, then pried George Gunton away from his wife and brought him and her sometimes eccentric but always independent ideas of life to Hot Springs.   It is hard to recall much about Gunton; just being the husband of such a woman as Mrs. Gunton was distinction enough for any but the most unusual of men, and Gunton was hardly that.   He wore a magnificent black beard, perhaps thereby endeavoring to establish his virility.   Not long after the Guntons arrived they had a visitor, Marcus, Baron Rosenkrantz, a direct lineal descendant of the Rosenkrantz in Hamlet.   The Baron was a soldier of fortune who had led an eventful life.   He had received a splendid education at a university, which he kept alive by being an omnivorous reader.   He knew more about more different things than any man I have ever met, almost all of which was absolutely wrong.   He had an amazing facility for drawing wrong conclusions from given facts but could always point to the page and line of some authority to support his conclusions. In the course of a varied career, from hobnobbing with the great and near great to being a billiard marker in Atlantic City, he had accumulated a fund of stories about most of the prominent men and women of the world, nearly all cynical and, if he could so turn them, salacious. With all, he was a charming conversationalist and companion if you did not take him seriously. He had quixotic streaks of idealism, as when, against public opinion, he came to the rescue of a colored girl who had deserted an unwelcome baby in rather distressing circumstances. Perhaps this was partly because the Baron loved a row. He always had a lawsuit or two pending.

Once I came home from a winter in Florida which had culminated in my catching whooping cough from my children. By the time I was back I was completely innocuous but the Baron pretty nearly made a pariah of me with his stories.

The rumor was that the Baron came on this visit hoping Mrs. Gunton might be tiring of Mr., knowing she had considerable money and gambling on the chance that he might be a successor. His plans went awry when he fell in love with Rebe English and she with him. They were married and only a few years later both Mr. and Mrs. Gunton died, leaving the house to Rebe, which she christened "Roseloe."

From then until her death Rebe Rosenkrantz dominated social life at Hot Springs. I started to write that she became a social arbiter but no one so little a snob and as kindly, sympathetic and honest as Rebe could have an epithet implying a tendency to lay down the law. Both she and Marcus were splendid hosts, providing good food, good liquor, and good company of all sorts and always interesting.  While they gave small dinners, their specialty was Sunday luncheons, at times with over fifty people, young and old.  Roseloe commands a sweeping view and in October nothing was ever finer than eating and thereafter playing cards on the veranda overlooking the mountains covered with nature's tapestry.  There was bridge for those who wanted it, high stakes or low as one might choose, and plenty of good talk if you didn't want bridge.  You could even stroll into the Baron's extraordinary library of erotica if so inclined.

Rebe did much for the Valley.  Annually she used to arrange a putting tournament for the benefit of the Visiting Nurse Association and, while I never heard her ask for a contribution, the amount of money she raised was amazing, the largest individual source of income for that charity.

At the end the Baron developed tuberculosis and died.  Rebe lived a few years longer but though she had inherited a considerable fortune it had not been sufficient to support the Baron indefinitely and her last years were tragic.  She finally died of cancer, dependent on loyal friends for any comforts.

Seth Barton French, one of the Morgan partners, built the first elaborate place in Hot Springs, the house now owned and vastly improved by Mrs. A. Kelly Evans, on the side of Little Mountain overlooking The Homestead.  French did not live long to enjoy his home, and after his death Mrs. French lived here for a time.  The house was rented for two years to Andrew Mellon, when Secretary of the Treasury, and for some years to Mrs. Dunlop, until she married Archie McCrea and they bought the famous old colonial Carter's Grove in Tide-water Virginia. Shortly after they left Mrs. Evans bought the place.

French was very much of a character while he lived here. Portly and red-faced, he used to puff around a few holes of golf but mostly sat by the first tee and gossiped. One day, telling of his fishing camp near Newport, he said his fish cost him some staggering amount per pound, I believe five dollars. A youngster on the outskirts of the circle heard this and made a remark which to his discomfiture was overheard: "Gee, that's nothing. We hired a team, drove thirty-six miles to Marlinton on the Greenbrier, fished two days and drove back. We only got two bass, neither weighing as much as half a pound. Guess our fish cost us at least ten times as much per pound as his."

That was quite a trip anyway. To save the horses, the drive, both coming and going, was made by night. Sleeping quarters in Marlinton were something only youth could take. The river was really too big to wade and we could not get a boat. We caught no fish and it was no wonder that the driver, one of the fishermen, fell asleep coming down Back Creek Mountain. By the grace of God the horses turned into the bank on the right with no damage other than a rather rude awakening for two of the party who were gently deposited on the clay.

My father built a house which was soon discarded and replaced with the one known today as "Fairacre." Decatur Axtell built the house now called the "Pink Cottage." Dr. Carl Brandt built a part of Edgewood Cottage, afterwards sold to Dr. Robertson, who enlarged it before selling it to my sister-in-law and her husband, the George Warringtons.

The influx of those seeking homes in the Valley which started in those early days has continued on down to the present. Besides those mentioned above, the Harrison family of Cincinnati built a large bungalow, "The Chestnuts," and Julius Walsh "The Patch." The last really elaborate house was that of George Ellis, adjoining McKee Dunn's at the entrance to Dunn's Gap. Mrs. Ellis, with a wonderful flair for making things grow, has succeeded in transplanting successfully laurel, rhododendron and azalea from native plants and has about the grounds one of the finest collections of English box in the State of Virginia. Most of the desirable sites in the Valley have been purchased and in recent years many who have fallen in love with the country tapped by the Road have bought farms farther away though within commuting distance of Hot Springs, particularly along the Jackson and Cowpasture Rivers.

# 8. *Why the Springs are Hot*

**D**URING one of the early summers at Hot Springs, Nathaniel Shaler, Professor of Geology at Harvard, made extended visits. Although I cannot find the records, I believe he had been employed by the Railway Company to make a survey of coal resources along the line. Between trips he stayed with us at Ingallston. Shaler, besides being an outstanding authority in his field, was a great humanist. Later on at Harvard I took his course, Geology 4, which was at that time a "snap" course; I suppose that was one of the

reasons I selected it, although memory of the summer at
Hot Springs influenced the choice. Like others who may
have had equally frivolous reasons, I was richly rewarded.
I had heard that members of the faculty remonstrated
with Shaler because he did not make his students work
hard enough or hew strictly to the line of the subject he
was teaching but, be that as it may, you could not listen
to him lecture twice a week without absorbing cultural
background far beyond what might have come from
more conventional instruction. The study of the earth
on which we live has ramifications leading into almost
every form of human activity and Shaler never hesitated
if he wanted to wander afield in his talks.

M. E. Ingalls found Shaler a kindred spirit and in
nothing more than the mutual liking for tramping over
hills and through the woods. I don't think there was any
idea of discovering commercial deposits of minerals in
the neighborhood of Hot Springs but, just because he
liked the country, while staying with us, Shaler, with my
father, spent the days rambling about. There were times
when father could not go and then I tagged along with
Shaler. Apparently he liked young people and, as is so
often the case with true scientists, enjoyed opening the
eyes of youth to the world about. From these walks I
absorbed quite a bit of knowledge of local geology.

The roots of the Appalachians are those of ancient
mountains, ancient even in terms of geologic time. The
first mountains were eroded down in the course of eons
of time to a flat plain, then the land uplifted and new
valleys cut to make the present formation. From the
top of Warm Springs Mountain the ridges, rising in
serried ranks on each side, are approximately at the same
level; these ridges mark the surface of the ancient plain.
Naturally the plain was not absolutely level but had

rivers and streams meandering through it. As the land rose the beds of these streams were deepened, the genesis of our valleys.

In the nineties the extent of the continental ice sheet was not as well determined as it has been since and one thing I recall Shaler looking for was evidence of glaciation near Hot Springs, not by the great ice sheet but by local glaciers. One of these, he suggested, once filled the Warm Springs Valley, to be succeeded, as it melted, by a great river, perhaps fed from the melting ice sheet farther to the north. The river undoubtedly existed but the possibility of a local glacier has been pretty well eliminated by later studies. It was this river which filled the valley with the clay and immense boulders which were to give so much trouble when later on foundations were sunk for the tower.

Shaler also gave me the explanation of our hot springs, which I believe is still generally accepted. Throughout this area there are many instances of dykes of igneous material extruded through the strata of sedimentary rock. Of these the most spectacular is Sounding Knob, about thirty-five miles northeast of Hot Springs, on Jack Mountain, an extension of Warm Springs Mountain. This dyke juts up about two hundred and fifty feet through a flat on top of the mountain and is perhaps two hundred feet in diameter. A hair-raising road winds around this granite mass, on top of which is a high fire tower. If the rock on which this tower stands is struck it gives off a ringing sound, hence the name.

The supposition is that these dykes are composed of ferrous material with relatively high power of heat conductivity. Their roots are in the hot interior of the earth and they carry the heat toward the surface. When these dykes were upthrust the strata through which they were forced were shattered and fractured. Surface rain water, working its way down into the earth, meets these fractures and gradually seeps along them until it comes to the dyke. There it is warmed and, flowing upward along the dyke, in consequence, comes to the surface as a hot spring. This water at some time in its travels is subject to great heat and dissolves various chemicals from the rocks it passes through, so that on reaching the surface it is not only hot but highly mineralized. If you want to know how much mineral it carries don't bother with a laboratory test but ask the plumbers who have to maintain the bathhouse piping how long it takes to fill a pipe with deposits, particularly if it is for overflow, where the water cools and can no longer hold the minerals in solution.

There must be such dykes near the various hot springs here but none are apparent near the outflow. The probabilities are that they come to the surface of the old river bed and are covered by hundreds of feet of clay and detritus, the water gradually having dissolved channels through this to the surface.

While there are other theories of the origin of the hot springs, this seems to be generally accepted today. Sometimes people fear that through blasting or other disturbance of the valley floor the springs may be lost but from the above explanation it is pretty obvious that the chance of anything of this sort occurring is remote indeed.

In the course of these rambles we learned that it was possible to go to the top of the mountain in front of the hotel and walk along the ridge north to where the highway crossed. There wasn't much of a path and most of the way was a scramble or climb up and over rocks.

Just before coming to the highway the trail led to Flag Rock. The present Skyline Drive drops below that pinnacle, going around it. This pinnacle, while by no means the highest point on Warm Springs Mountain (in fact, surveys show it is lower than the flat right above The Homestead), stands out, as the ridge falls away to the north to the highway pass and is lower to the south for a mile or more, allowing a view in every direction. Pollard, in his description of this part of the country, published in 1870, speaks of the pinnacle as Flag Rock, and the tradition that it was a signal station in the Civil War is probably correct. From that point can be seen Panther Gap, the break in North Mountain, one of the barriers of the Alleghanies on the northern side of the Shenandoah through which troops going west had to move, and they could undoubtedly have been picked up there fifteen or twenty miles away. On the west the site commands a view of the Huntersville Pike, coming up through Warm Springs Gap from West Virginia. Troop movements through the Warm Springs Valley, in the innumerable Shenandoah Valley campaigns, were frequent and Flag Rock would have been a natural viewpoint for warning. In any event, until quite recently a flag was kept flying from its top, by whose efforts I have never learned.

Flag Rock became an important point for our family. Within a year or two of our first walk there my father established it as the place to celebrate his birthday, on September sixth, and until he died in 1914 woe betide any member of the Ingalls clan who failed to attend the supper there. Shep, for so many years the guardian angel of the Homestead bar, then of the Japanese Room and in the end, until his death, of the Homestead Club, superintended the catering, and the suppers, cooked on the spot, were delicious indeed. Of course corn was roasted in the huge fire, there was watermelon and the like, but the chief dish was smothered chicken. Much as I like to cook I never quite solved Shep's recipe. The chicken was first broiled over an ember fire just enough to char the skin, then put in a flat, covered pan and steamed. This is where the magic came in. Shep claimed it could only be done by using champagne to generate the steam, and that is what he used with other secret ingredients. Later I endeavored to pry the secret from him. Shep said he thought ginger ale would do as well; I tried that, but never had the fortitude or purse to try champagne and perhaps that is why I universally failed.

At these picnics champagne was not used solely for cooking. Shep had his "band," and of course someone would essay a *pas seul*, inspired by the firelight without and the firewater within. The ground was never leveled off nor the sweet fern and blueberry bushes cut away and in the many years we went to Flag Rock many distinguished jurists, bankers and politicians, who found the altitude somehow affected their sense of balance, had to be rescued from the bushes. Once, when halfway down the mountain on the way home, I was sent back in a "runabout" to look for a financier who was missing from the party, to find him peacefully sleeping with head on a bed of fern.

## 9. *The Red Gods Travel the Road*

HOT SPRINGS was growing lustily and on the whole peacefully when a calamity struck which might easily have written finis to the venture. The destruction of The Homestead by fire had a peculiarly dramatic aspect for me.

That spring, my freshman year in college, I had tried to row though with nothing to offer except considerable brawn and great willingness. The coach put seven others like myself into a boat and by brute force and persistence we managed to make it tough for some of the boats with

more competent oarsmen. One day in late May the coach
ordered a brush with one of these boats. We were doing
nobly when just before the finish I had a terrible cramp.
We got back to the float and they had to get a cab to take
me to my room. The health of a boy in college was not
so carefully looked after in those days and I didn't know
of any doctor. Old Eckert, the famous janitor of Beck Hall,
produced a Cambridge Irishman who shot me full of
morphine and left me. I only know by hearsay what
happened during the next three weeks but fortunately
they got me into the hands of Maurice Richardson, a
wonderful surgeon, who operated after telling my father
there was not much chance, with a three-day-old burst
appendix.

When I could be moved my father took his car to Boston
and brought me to Hot Springs on a stretcher. I still had
an open wound, weighed about 110 pounds against the
185 I checked in with for that last row, and could just
get around but not up or down stairs. On the night of
July second my nurse had dressed the wound and put me
to bed. Sometime later, about eleven o'clock, I was
wakened by people running about but before I was
oriented my father came into the room with the butler and
said, "We've got to get you out of here. The hotel is on
fire and, with embers flying all about, this house may
catch at any moment." They carried me down and put
me in a steamer chair on the lawn in front of the
house. By that time you could see the building only when
a gust from the maelstrom of fire swept the smoke and
flames aside for a moment. It was a perfectly clear, still
night, which made it possible to save the casino and bathhouse. Hanging in the sky was a full moon and rising
higher than Little Mountain was a column of flames and
smoke. The old hotel was sheathed with pine and many of

the timbers had been seasoning and drying for almost a hundred and fifty years. The roar of the flames was continuous but I felt rather than heard the noise. Ever so often there would come a crash or dull boom and a mass of flames would boil up, carrying burning sticks into the murk above. From time to time someone would come back to see that everything was safe at the house and report to me. The hotel was only partially full but even at that it was a miracle that everyone got out uninjured. No one ever knew how the fire originated, perhaps from a defective or overheated kitchen stack where this went through the roof, or possibly defective wiring. In any event the fire burned down from the top, which probably accounts for people getting out safely.

That was a busy night, with every odd bed in Hot Springs in use to take care of the evicted guests. Practically no one saved their clothes. It may be for that reason that surprisingly few left Hot Springs. People were moved into the Virginia, where the kitchen and dining room immediately began to function, and the local stores did a thriving business in all sorts of apparel.

The next day I managed to get down to view the ruins, a great black hole with little specks of fire here and there and jutting up from this some chimneys and a few water pipes dripping senseless little trickles, where bathroom fixtures had hung. I was being pushed about in a wheel chair and we came across a fine-looking old gentleman poking in the embers with a stick. When I tried to speak to him he turned away rather churlishly. Two or three days later I saw him again and he came up all smiles. I said something about his getting over the shock. He laughed and said, "Oh, that! It was nothing, and in these blue jeans and jumper over underclothes, I couldn't get a shirt, I'm really comfortable. But I lost my false teeth; I remembered throwing them out the window and, sure enough today I found them right under where my window was. Now, I'm all right."

The fire which destroyed The Homestead on July 2, 1901, might easily have put an end to growth in the Valley. Stagnating in 1889, it was my father's advent which brought new life. His personality dominated all that was done for twenty-three years and is so important that anyone who wishes to know how and why Hot Springs became what it is must understand him.

He and I were very close. Perhaps this was because I was the youngest of four sons and quite a bit younger than any of the others, so that at the end of his life when my father had more leisure for his family I was always around, but, in addition, we had minds which worked much the same way. The second generation did not have the drive of the first, of course; I doubt if I would have had the courage which enabled him to break away from a rocky Maine farm. His family had exhausted its resources in educating his two older brothers to be physicians and he was scheduled to work the farm. One day he was picking stones from a hillside and, stopping for lunch, came to the conclusion that although he did not mind the hard work the prospect of picking stones from the same eroding hillside every year for the rest of his life was something he could not contemplate. He determined to break away and get an education on his own. He did that and although he was unable to complete his course at Bowdoin, where he matriculated, he succeeded in graduating from the Harvard Law School.

In this crisis over the fire everything he did was long and carefully discussed with me.

My father had immense drive and force. Perhaps he was a bit of an egoist as well, which may have been necessary if he was to have enough self-confidence to accomplish all he did. These qualities made it difficult for him to have many close friends and his intimacies were few. He did have the power of inspiring amazing loyalty and confidence among those who worked with him.

Two anecdotes, expressive of the difficult nature of his personality, are worth recalling. The first occurred a year or two after the fire:

We had finished luncheon and Father was going to take a nap, as was his custom before the second eighteen holes of the day. Before lying down he went over to the desk, wrote out a telegram and handed it to me with instructions to send it.

Now a word is in order as to my father's chirography. Its only recommendation was that the banks always seemed to recognize the signature. He claimed that he once wrote a beautiful hand and I have seen samples of a perfectly conventional Spencerian script. However, the way of a young student was hard and he had eked out meagre means to get through the Harvard Law School by copying pension rolls at so much a name. I don't know how long it took to change the Spencerian correctness for what later passed as handwriting but if the change came before he was through they must have needed handwriting experts in the pension office.

I barged off promptly to the telegraph office and pushed the blank across the counter, to have the clerk look at it and remark, "Fay, I can't read it. What does it say?"

I looked, and that was that. I was in a predicament. First, I did not want to disturb the old man and, second, I hated to admit I could not read what he had written. Yet it might be important. I went back to the house but before going in made three circuits, then took a deep breath, walked in and over to his couch, shook his shoulder and said, "Father, I didn't send that telegram." "Huh, what?" he ejaculated, sitting up. "Why?" "Because I couldn't read it," I said. I held the offending blank out and he grabbed it. Then, the only time I ever saw him abashed, he said, "Neither can I. Give me another blank."

The other occurred a few years later. I had bummeled through college, taking nothing too seriously and rather bored with the whole thing. The first two years I took some extra courses as a safety measure in case I failed in one, and at the end of my sophomore year discovered I could get my degree in three years if I wished. Father thought I should if possible and as a stimulus told me that if I got honor marks the next year he would make a trip to Egypt, Greece and Italy the following winter and take me along. It worked out all right and we made the trip. Coming from Greece to Italy we landed at Brindisi and wanted to go straight to Rome. There were some English people on the boat from Patras who suggested that we join up to get a private car and avoid a change at Naples. This was done and all went swimmingly until we got to Ventimiglia, just outside of Naples, when our car was put on a side-track and we had the humiliation of seeing one after another Rome Express go by while we waited; they were not going to haul a private car on any but the slowest local train. My father became more and more angry. A gang of section hands was working where we were parked and, they being the nearest available representatives of the railway organization, Father got out of the car and began to remonstrate with them. In imagination I can still see their kindly smiles and hear their "Si, si, signor" while my father became more and more exasperated. I never knew before the wealth of his vocabulary of invective. He was beaten and he knew it but even the English with us did not dare smile when he climbed back into the car.

To go back to Hot Springs, the morning after the fire my father wired Elzner and Anderson, the architects who had done most of the work on the alteration of The Homestead, to come immediately to Hot Springs and bring a contractor with them. They arrived the next day and departed that night. Before they left outlines for the rebuilding had been settled and orders placed for materials. It was no easy task. Insurance should have been adequate but the policies had errors in them and consequently more money had to be raised. By that time the railway had passed out of the hands of the syndicate and the syndicate had dissolved. New money had to be raised and a mortgage of $220,000 was put on the property, a considerable proportion of which had to be taken up by my father personally. This was all paid off in a few years.

The first portion of the hotel to be rebuilt was that now known as the main section, with a ballroom at the northeast corner. This main section was ready for occupancy the following spring and shortly afterwards the west wing was completed.

A few years after the fire there came a hiatus in my close connection with the Road. Immediately after graduating I began to practice law in New York and lived there with more or less infrequent visits to the Valley until I returned in 1922, after which I could answer as did the mountaineer when asked if he had lived where he was all his life, "Not yit." On one of these visits my wife and I drove down the Road proudly in our first automobile, a chain-driven Locomobile, and incidentally the noisiest motor car I have ever seen or heard. I was only casually aware of all that was happening at Hot Springs and we roared up to the door of Ingallscote about ten o'clock at night after a rather adventurous trip. We were a bit miffed at our welcome, which did not seem so spontaneous as usual. After we had gone to our room Mother knocked and said I must not be offended if my father seemed put out about something. "This is the first time an automobile has ever been driven to our front door." We had dropped right into the midst of a great automobile war!

Father put up a good fight to keep them away but of course it was a losing one as it has been at Bar Harbor and Bermuda. Leading the van for the motorists was old Dr. Pole. My father became very fond of the doctor and, when he began to break up, trusted him implicitly, but this automobile business almost started a feud. The old doctor was very much of a personality. Good physician that he was, he had to have his moments of relaxation and once in a while he would come roaring into Hot Springs and liven up the place. An automobile was a natural for such occasions and it was inevitable that he should come into conflict with my father.

When we arrived that night the anti-motorists had lost every battle except the drive up to Ingallscote. Next morning I drove the car behind a bush on the lawn and didn't start it until we left, as unobtrusively as possible, at seven in the morning.

The automobile war still rumbles a bit now, thirty-five years later. Until quite recently it raged about the roads through Dunn's Gap and the Cascades. The last ditch of the conservatives are the riding and driving trails, now widened so a car might go through them except for some nasty concrete posts just high enough to snag the front axle but low enough so a surrey or buckboard can go over.

## 10. Some Who Have Lived
## Along the Road

WHEN the bathhouse was completed in 1892 it was staffed by men and women brought over from the Scandinavian countries of Europe. Hot Springs has been favored with many breaks of fortune and not the least of these was the character and personality of these people. In the beginning they flocked together but as time went on they became more and more a real part of the community.

One of the first and in many ways the most remarkable was Carl Hillman, a masseur, who died only a few years ago. I have hardly known anyone who left more friends, not only at Hot Springs but scattered over America. He was loved, not for his skill but for his character and personality. All of these Scandinavians were grand specimens of the northern race. They loved the out-of-doors and soon began to acquire camps along the rivers near-by, where they erected shelters for their interminable picnics and outings. Of these, Hillman's was the most noteworthy. An invitation to one of his parties was something to envy and the consequent party long to be remembered.

Giving such a party was a ritual for Hillman. If asked what time to arrive he would reply, "Any time. We'll eat about six-thirty, but come early and fish or swim. I'm going about noon." He didn't really mean he would go at noon; he meant that at that time he would begin his preparations. He had a fearful and wonderful collection of gadgets, such as grills, ice boxes and what-nots which had to be assembled and packed just so. On one typical occasion I arrived around five and found perhaps twenty people there. On seeing me, Hillman rushed over with the greeting, "Come, you must have a drink!" He walked off, returning in a minute or so with a tiny glass, probably a half-ounce jigger, with a wee drappie of whiskey and liberal water. "Skoal!" he cried, and we downed the liquor. From then on until the party broke up, at intervals of five or ten minutes there came occasion for another skoal, it might be the arrival of a guest, a story that had just occurred to Hillman, one of the kind you can't tell the next night at dinner but told with an inimitable chuckle, in perfect English with just enough vestige of foreign accent to add to its charm, or it might be that Hillman wanted you to try another of the myriad Swedish hors d'oeuvres spread out on the long table. You never seemed to take a real drink but somehow those innumerable "skoals" had a cumulative effect. Alcohol taken in this way apparently results in a sort of crescendo to the life of a party but is apt to be a bit insidious in its effects. On this party my brother, George, who then was one of the New York Central vice presidents, had taken with him two prominent New York officials of a steel company. These men got back to The Homestead somewhat the worse for wear, much to the disgust of their wives. I overheard one trying to justify himself the next day, saying, "I really don't understand what happened. I'm sure I didn't have one real drink all evening." "Maybe," replied his wife, "but how did it happen that I'm told you insisted on stopping at the first ford on the way home, taking a flashlight and trying to catch a trout in your hands." (That was just after "Tol'able David" was filmed here.)

Of course, the hors d'oeuvres were only what the name implies and there was plenty of good, substantial food as well, beefsteaks, chicken, corn and perhaps some odd dishes. Cooking was Hillman's hobby and he liked things well flavoured. I remember once he got a wild turkey about Thanksgiving and saved it for Christmas, *not on ice.* Hillman thought it was fine. He loved to fish and shoot but actually his love for these things was like his love for cooking. They did not mean much to him except as an opportunity for human companionship, and for that he had an unsurpassed genius. Always gentle and tolerant, with an irrepressible sense of humor, for which his own misadventures, and they were many, were as often as not the butt, it was a delight to be with him. Hillman was an independent soul and, while living and practicing here, he went his own way.

Hillman was only one of this group who first and last gave so much to Hot Springs. Most of them are gone now but the son of one, Carl Wallin, is the chief engineer for the Company, carrying on in the old tradition. Carl's father died a number of years ago and his mother in 1947. At the moment of writing this volume, the Nursing Association is in the throes of rebuilding its hospital and Carl Wallin, as a tribute to his mother, has volunteered his services. While he makes no claims as an architect, the design, and a most attractive one, is his work and he is also giving his time to the supervision of the construction.

When Chris Andersen came to The Homestead as manager in 1917 he fell naturally into this group and his camp on the Cowpasture, by the oxbow surrounding the farm which James S. Knowlson, of Chicago, later bought and developed, was for years one of the best and most used.

It was in the late nineties, too, that Tate Sterrett, a member of a prominent family in Rockbridge County, came along the Road to the Valley through Buffalo Gap, to take charge of the Homestead Stables. Shortly afterward he acquired Fassifern Farm and that reached the height of its glory during his life. Tate was a magnificent figure of a man. Well over six feet, with ruddy complexion and inclined to be stout, he always wore a ten-gallon hat and dressed the part of a horseman. He was a real sportsman and loved to hunt and shoot. He established a pack of hounds at Fassifern and, while the hunt was more or less informal, it was a really sporting pack.

Horse racing came early to the Valley. It is said that the plateau on McKee Dunn's river farm was the first race track west of the Blue Ridge. At Fassifern there was another plateau where races had been held and Tate revived the sport. I don't think he cared much for flat racing, but for a number of years he arranged what were called steeple chases though these were more truly point to points. What made these original was that for some three or four hundred yards the course was so flagged that the horses had to go up the bed of the river. There are still pictures of these races hanging in the house at Fassifern, showing the horses splashing along; the winner was always the one who made the best time through the water part of the course.

Tate also bought the Oaks, a lovely old house on the Road between the Hot and the Warm, where his son's widow now lives. For a short while after he got the Oaks he operated a sort of tavern there but it never became as famous as Fassifern. Miss Sally (now formally Mrs. Mines) came to Fassifern while Tate was alive and still presides there, serving up the fried chicken, country ham, spoon bread and baked apples. She has the old registers and you can read where John D. Rockefeller and Henry Ford had a luncheon party. What memories these old registers bring back to those who knew the Valley in the old days!

Incidentally, it was about the turn of the century that Mr. Rockefeller made his many visits to Hot Springs. There are rather amusing stories of his encounters with the natives, and his bright new dimes. He and my mother got along famously, and she often took him on her almost daily drives about the country. At one picnic I was a bit awed by the old gentleman, but nothing of that sort ever disturbed my mother, who ordered him around as brusquely and directly as she did me. It was John D., Jr., however, who was the more frequent visitor.

Two famous physicians early took a keen interest in Hot Springs, S. Weir Mitchell and Francis Delafield. They both came often and made long stays although, to the best of my knowledge and belief, never practiced here. It used to be said, however, that half the people who came to The Homestead during the summer were patients of one or the other and were sent here by them. Weir Mitchell was a man of culture and varied interests. In the account of golf I have mentioned his friendship for Herbert Beauclerk and that he built a cottage for him here.

It was at Dr. Delafield's suggestion that the old, steep path up Warm Springs Mountain was relocated to give a uniform grade of one in ten. He had signposts put up, giving distance from the hotel and rise in elevation, which, or their replacements, still stand. This path was later made into the driving road which goes to the airport. The purpose of the doctor's path was not to get anywhere but to permit of controlled exercise. After the one in ten grade had been established for two miles and a rise of 1,050 feet attained, the alignment of the old path was left for the balance of the way. When made into a road, another reason for stopping at that point became apparent. It then ran into the almost precipitous rock wall of the mountain, and consequent difficulties. When the road was built there was nothing to do but blast a way on. The Company had a dynamite man named Saunders who handled the explosive. He was one of the old-fashioned kind who believed the success of a blast was determined by the amount of dynamite detonated at one time and the volume of noise produced; clearing away the rock was just an incidental. Saunders also had a tremendous voice and loved to give warning of a blast. Many times I have been about to putt when I'd hear from almost a mile away his cry of "FIR-R-R-R-R-R-E" followed by a rumble which echoed back and forth across the Valley for what seemed minutes; then a huge cloud of dust would billow over the mountain. Almost as much dynamite was used as there was rock dislodged and, even at that, a few hundred yards of steep pitch was never eliminated.

It was during this time that Amelie Rives, later the Countess Troubetskoy, made many visits to the Valley, as a result of which she wrote "Tanis the Sang-Digger," a novel with a beautiful description of the life in these mountains before the coming of progress with a capital P.

Julia Marlowe spent at least two summers at The Homestead. She was a woman of great charm and gave freely of her talents for the entertainment of those here. One summer she brought with her a protegee who later became quite a famous musical comedy actress. Julia Marlowe arranged sundry entertainments at which this girl, who shall be nameless, gave performances. Now I was a bit too young to look at Marlowe except from a distance, but this girl was about my own age or a bit younger. I was old enough, however, to feel the glamour of the stage and, watching Marlowe, find her bewitching. What more natural than that I should attribute all I imagined about Marlowe to this protegee, and set right out to make an impression and learn firsthand what these women of the stage had which others did not. Perhaps it was a fortunate experience for me for never afterwards did I have any desire to meet off the boards any actresses, and there were quite a few whom I worshiped on the stage and to see whom I spent more than I should of a quite generous allowance, going back again and again for repeat performances. The protegee proved to be a rather dull, stuffy little prig. From then on I never dared hazard another disillusion and preferred my idols safely the other side of the footlights. Probably I didn't appreciate the artistic temperament.

Old Dr. Pole came to the Valley in 1882, building himself a house on the Road where Valley View now stands. Amelie Rives took him as the hero for her book, "Tanis the Sang-Digger" and he deserved the niche she carved for him. He had trained for dentistry but shifted to medicine and came here, I understood, because he felt his health would not stand city life. He was a natural physician and through the many years he practiced here acquired a knowledge of the possibilities of the spa which was unequalled. Perhaps some of his theories might be considered unorthodox today but he got results.

Dr. Pole had a large family. His son, Edgar, a brilliant man, took over his practice in time; perhaps his brilliance approached the erratic, but he had many fascinating and attractive facets.

Another of Dr. Pole's sons, Lanier, also practiced medicine at Hot Springs. He had as fine a mind as his brother, Edgar, and, beyond that, was gifted with human sympathy and understanding of the sort that makes for great physicians. He was beloved by everyone in the Valley, and the work he did to better living conditions for the rural population cannot be exaggerated. It so happened that the women of the Garden Club at one time entered a contest to make a miniature mountain home and Lanier and I worked together many evenings, making for them such things as picket fences out of matches and over 3,000 shingles for the roof. I was lost in admiration for his deft fingers, as well as for the well-rounded man I came to know. Unfortunately, death cut him off early.

Ed Porter was an indigenous product of the Valley. He came from the mountains but got an education, even matriculating at the University of Virginia. However, he scorned the shams and trappings of sophistication and made himself into a moving picture model of a mountaineer. I recall once being summoned as a character witness in a suit involving a negro. In Virginia witnesses cannot remain in the courtroom during a trial before they have testified. I sat on the courthouse steps waiting to testify, where I found Ed Porter, called for the same purpose. I had known him for some years but not so well then as later. Ed was about six feet, two or three and cadaverous. He had a moth-eaten red beard and always dressed as if he had just come out of the woods. Seeking to be a bit facetious, I said to him, "I don't see why they called you as a witness; I've always heard you are the biggest liar in Bath County." Ed slowly unlocked his various joints, stood upright and looked me straight in the eye. I got a bit nervous. I had remembered "the Virginian's" remark and smiled as I made my quip, but Ed had somewhat of a violent reputation and you don't call a man a liar in the mountains, even in fun, without being prepared to take the consequences. I began to wonder what these would be. Ed pointed a long, bony finger at me and said with perfect solemnity, "'Tain't so, Fay. Not so long as Howard McClintic lives. While he's around I'm only the second greatest."

Ed eventually moved from the Valley and acquired a fine farm on the Cowpasture, about fifteen miles away. Among other things the farm raised a number of coveys of quail. I used to go over to shoot and enjoyed Ed, I believe, as much as the shooting, which is saying a lot. A few years later when we began to develop the Cascades stream for fishing we put several restrictions on permits to fish, among others that fish could only be taken on artificial flies. Ed sent word he wanted to fish and I sent him a standard permit. I heard nothing from him until just before the opening of the quail season, when a mutual friend came into the office and said he had a message for me from Ed. "Ed told me to tell you you were welcome to shoot as usual but you had to use a 22-caliber rifle. He calculates that is just as fair as giving him a permit to catch trout with a fly." The drinks were certainly on me, and next year I sent him a permit with all restrictions marked out. But he was a true sport. He turned up with a can full of worms but used none of them and quit fishing after he had taken a few less fish than our rules permitted.

Ed Porter was crude, not always too neat, and sometimes considered a bit of a blatherskite. However, anyone who hated sham as he did commands respect. He told a story at a luncheon he had for us when Rachel took the Bath County Hounds to hunt across the river from his farm, which, as he told it, was well worth preserving. That was a great luncheon anyway. I do not recall how many we were but I was there with two friends who looked for quail in the morning, while Rachel, with a small field, took out the hounds. I believe they had a run on the foothills of Rough Mountain but did not kill. It was a chilly day and we came to lunch with sharp appetites. This was in the days of prohibition and, to start things off, Ed gave us some brandy. He told us it was distilled from wine which he had made out of a particular lot of wild grapes, growing back in the mountains, of which he alone knew; then, he said, he had given this wine to the only man he knew who still preserved the ancient art of moonshining and aging liquor. The drink was both potent and excellent. At that date the only open season for game was quail, but we had wild turkey, venison and grouse. Mrs. Porter provided delicious preserves, and even our sharpened appetites came off second best in the contest with the feast set before us.

After lunch the talk naturally turned to hunting. Ed asked if I had heard the story of the two coon hunts he had staged for a certain prominent New Yorker. I had heard the story but let him tell it again for the benefit of the crowd. The event happened a number of years ago before Ed got his farm on the Cowpasture. He did not care much for the man who wanted the hunt but said the man's wife was a thoroughbred. They caught a couple of coons and the evening was a success in every way. About two or three years later this same man returned to Hot Springs and wanted another hunt. Ed was all for it, but when the party assembled he discovered there was a new wife. Ed's characterization of her was decidedly unprintable. The man in question had a lot of money and Ed was sure that was why she married him. Ed said he was nauseated the way she lovey-doveyed the man, squealed every time she stepped over a log and was enthusiastic about all the wrong things. Finally Ed's old coon hound gave tongue and they started after.

"I knew it wasn't rightly a coon, but that woman kept giggling and making such a fuss I let 'em go after the dog. We came up to him, his head in one end of a hollow log. The old hound backed out, looked at me and started to leave but I sicked him on. Then I told that woman, 'That there dog has a coon in the log. You go to that end with your gun and I'll shoo him out to you.' I held the dog so he couldn't leave, then grabbed a bunch of dried grass, touched a match to it and stuck it into the log. It made the God-damnedest smell you ever knew. In about two shakes that coon came out of the other end, a black and white one with his tail high in the air, and right at that woman. She got a full chokebore load in the face. She had some fancy perfume on but you couldn't notice it any more. I don't think I ever enjoyed a coon hunt more. They never asked me to take them out again tho' I don't think she ever suspected just how it happened."

Ed is gone now but he has left two sons who carry on. They are a hardy breed. I went over a few years ago to shoot, on a raw November day. Going to the house first I found Andrew, one of the boys, sitting in front of the fire and as I came in he had his flannel shirt open and was examining the wound where his appendix had been taken out six days before. He bemoaned the fact that he could not go out with us and show us where the birds were. About two hours later I saw him coming across the fields; he had not heard us shoot and wanted to tell us where to go. He hadn't bothered to put on a coat but had buttoned the flannel shirt. Sure enough he located the birds. The covey got up and I winged a bird which went down in a ditch half full of water. I took the dogs over and my springer began to scratch at a groundhog hole, pretty good evidence the bird had gone in there. Andrew did not want to leave a wounded bird any more than I did, but that hole might harbor a hibernating rattler and to reach in meant standing in water. Nothing daunted, Andrew climbed down and, sticking his arm in all the way to the shoulder, said he could feel the bird; a bit of squirming around and scratching at the opening and he brought it out. Andrew was covered with mud and at least half of him soaking wet, but he insisted on staying with us for quite a time and I never heard he was any the worse for the experience.

These mountain people are a sturdy lot anyway. Another good friend of mine was Nathan Bussard, who lived up in Highland County along the Road where it goes to Monterey. Bussard was really more of a friend of Dr. Hornbarger, my favorite shooting companion, than mine but I like to think he accepted me as well. Up in Big Valley, where he lived, the country has the same defects which bothered one of the border patrol who guarded the Japs. I asked this fellow if it was not God's country and he replied, "Perhaps, but God made an awful mistake when he made these hills and did not put in escalators."

Bussard had a number of coveys on his place and Hornbarger and I used to shoot there. As soon as we appeared Bussard would drop what he was doing, shucking corn, ploughing or whatever, and go along with us to show where the birds were. They were usually 'way up near the top of the mountain on one side or the other of the valley. Bussard was a heavy set man, on the shady side of sixty when I first knew him. He would start right up the hill with us at his heels. I wasn't what might be called a weakling but Bussard would set a pace so fast that I not only could not keep up but had great difficulty getting enough breath to ask some question which would necessitate his stopping to answer, thus giving me a chance to cease puffing.

These hill folk expect to get about on shank's mare and hills don't seem to count. There is a man, still working for the Company, who used to live in the Deeds Country, the wilderness on the eastern slope of Warm Springs Mountain, and daily walked to and from work, ten miles each way, climbing directly over the mountain in the process. They begin early, too. Today many thumb rides but in the early days of golf some caddies walked seven miles along the Road to the first tee, caddied for thirty-six holes and then walked home at night. It seems to be mostly a matter of getting used to it and then never being in a hurry—the latter comes naturally to any mountaineer.

## *11. The Road's Tributaries*

THERE is a certain nostalgia for the days when trips about the country on horseback or in horse-drawn vehicles made up so much of the life. People still drive horses at Hot Springs and great numbers ride the trails, but it is different now. Today people seem to want but a small amount of anything and the favorite drives are through the Cascades or Dunn's Gap and for riding they prefer The Homestead or Ritchie Trail, any of which can be covered in a short afternoon. Even for the trip to Fassifern, which is only ten miles, most people take a motor, while in the old days twenty miles to Gillett's and twenty miles back made just a comfortable day's horseback jaunt.

Of course the country has changed since Hot Springs was close to "backwoods" with plenty of farms within easy driving distance where the woman seldom left the place after she married. Untouched wilderness is still not far off, but the advent of the ubiquitous Ford, the improvement of all roads, centralized schools, and the occasional trip to town and the movies all have had their part in achieving the great aim of American society, to make everyone and everything just like everyone and everything else. Fortunately, it has not gone so far that you cannot still find log cabins nestled away amid old apple trees, with a few rose bushes scattered in the yard, where the soap kettle hangs on its tripod, and where you will see the carcass of a hog when frosty days come along. But the owner, even if his hills are so steep the plow will slide home after working a mountain meadow, likely as not is as familiar with the latest movie as the reader.

In the old days one could get on a horse without an objective and when dusk came to the hollows stop at a cabin and ask to be put up for the night. Perhaps you might be hospitably treated now if your car broke down but the sort of experiences I had can never come again. I remember one in particular. Even in those days it was a firm tradition that the best fishing or shooting was always to be found at the most remote point. A friend and I left Hot Springs in an old-fashioned buggy, with our fishing tackle stowed away, to seek what we could find along the headwaters. We expected rough roads and perhaps difficult fords and had as motive power a mule which we knew would pull until the traces broke and would keep on going no matter how deep the water—but only at his own pace; many hickory shoots were frayed over his back on the trip. We came to our river, fished that evening and then stopped at the first clearing. As expected, we were cordially welcomed. The cabin was immaculately clean; a chicken was killed for supper, and we passed a pleasant evening. Come bedtime we were told we could sleep in a sort of attic second floor, while the family used the kitchen and other room on the ground floor. We passed a comfortable night on quilt-covered string beds and woke in the morning to feel the September chill in the air. My friend climbed down the ladder first and a bit later I followed. He and the other men folk were sitting at the table and I joined them. I had just acquired a turtle-neck sweater and pulled this on over my shirt and trousers.

Now, reader, have you any idea how big the hole in a 32 Winchester barrel looks when pointed right at you from five feet? I didn't before but I learned then and there. In his slow drawl the owner of the cabin remarked, even as he picked the rifle from a nail on the wall and pointed it at me, "Stranger, you're in my house and I don't aim to shoot till I count fifty but no man is goin' to insult my wife and daughter by comin' to breakfast with his shirt outside his pants." I didn't know how long it took me to realize what was going on but I remember that the latch on the yard gate would not open and I tore my pants getting over the pickets. I never made good in track events but if my time had been taken until I was around a bend in the road and could jump into a bunch of laurel I am sure I would have qualified for the Olympics. I lay there for what seemed hours, wondering how I was going to get out of the country with a whole skin. Then I heard our mule coming down the road and, peering carefully out, was thankful to see my friend in the buggy—alone. "Hist," I whispered, "what are we going to do?" He was a mean man, that friend, and it all struck him as funny, so funny he just looked at me and laughed. At last he told me it was all fixed up, ample apologies had been made, and he even brought me a piece of corn pone for breakfast. But we drove a number of miles before we started fishing again, and came home by another route. Today the women and men would un-doubtedly be eating at the same time in such a cabin, the girls might be wearing overalls or possibly shorts, and my sweater would be a source of envy for the boys.

Of course, all trips were not as far into the backwoods as this and more often than not they were mixed parties. A favorite was to Nimrod Hall on the Cowpasture River. The drive followed the Road over the Warm Springs Mountain, past Bath Alum and down the river; it was about twenty-five miles. Most of the party rode horses but always there was a surrey with a chaperon or two. Arriving at Nimrod Hall by dusk or later, there was time for a swim in the river after dark, and back to food which tasted as none does today. Sometimes the party spent the night, going home the next day; at others remained to fish, or went on, once as far as Natural Bridge; at other times the return was by Clifton Forge and McGraw's Gap, the latter a beautiful wild woods road, but little changed today.

In those days Nimrod Hall was run by an English-man named Watson. He was an inveterate fisherman and I recall, to my eternal shame, one day when he and I got in a boat at the Hall and floated down stream all day. When we pulled to the bank and climbed into the wagon waiting for us we not only loaded the boat into it but also ninety-five smallmouth bass and some thirty perch.

There are still fish in the river but I am afraid others like us are partially responsible for more skillful fishermen having at times barren days.

One time, while at Nimrod Hall, Watson took all out to see a stallion he had just bought, named King Cadmus. I don't recall the breeding of the horse or much about him except that he was dark brown. Watson boasted that he was going to "clean up" the Virginia tracks with him. My brother Albert was riding one of the most ungainly and strange-looking horses I have ever known, well named Query. Albert rode Query because he was a hard rider and that was one horse he had never succeeded in tiring or breaking down. He also rode him because no one else could or would ride the beast. He had a mouth like iron and had run away with innumerable people. When he ran away he did not bolt but just wouldn't stop; once he spent the morning between the Homestead mounting block and the tollgate, going just fast enough so the rider, Murray Forbes, of Boston, couldn't slide off and could only turn him. Anyway, Albert got old Query so he would go for him. After listening to Watson's boasting, Albert called us aside and said, "I don't think that Cadmus is so much horse. If he'll only make the race long enough I can beat him on Query." A match race was arranged, with the bets double or nothing for a two days' stay for a party of twenty at Nimrod Hall, the distance two miles and the date ten days off. The great day came at last and they started. The track was half a mile and the first time round Query was hardly in it, by the second round he was holding his own, and by the third Watson was beginning to use his whip on Cadmus. At the finish Query was in the lead by many lengths. Query would be running still if Albert had not managed to steer him off the track and into a hayfield, where he slipped off. Watson was a good sport and a fine time was had by all.

Trips to White Sulphur were also fun. Of course, there was better train service between the two places then than now, but no self-respecting youth or maiden would think of such a prosaic method of transportation. Today it is an hour by motor car, but in the nineties it was a good smart horse that could make the trip in a day. That it took an even better horse to come back the next day was no disadvantage for it gave a good excuse for a day of fun at the Old White. White Sulphur was certainly gay in those days. That was the time when a young man of good family and attractive appearance, who could dance and flirt acceptably, could get room and board for practically nothing. If you really want to know what it was like, read James Branch Cabell's books.

One trip was memorable. There were three boys who arrived at the White, after riding through a summer rainstorm for the last twenty miles, in such a bedraggled condition it took argument to get their disreputable selves into the hotel. Riding clothes could not be dried out in one day so they stayed over for a second night. The next day there was one of the famous morning Germans. That afternoon, when it was time to start back, some fifteen or twenty boys and girls from White Sulphur decided to ride part of the way home as an escort. The party was not too prompt getting off and it was dusk when, nearing Callaghan's, someone suggested stopping at the Rumbold's for a refresher and to say good-bye. The refresher was good; then someone discovered a couple of negroes who could play and sing, and unexpectedly it was too late to go on or back, and the whole party stayed at Rumbold's. Just where all slept remains a mystery; there were not enough beds and at least one boy did the best he could on a piazza, rolled up in a porch rug. It wasn't only the horses that were tired when the three musketeers drifted into Hot Springs the next afternoon.

But it was not only the long, overnight trips that were popular. Anything was an excuse for a picnic. The favorite sites were the grove at Falling Spring, the old mill by Groce's Spring at the foot of Dunn's Gap, Flag Rock and Bath Alum. The latter was a particular favorite for, while the hotel was not running, there was the ballroom and an old tinkly piano out of which Mary Howe could make music, as she still can from the most unlikely apparatus as well as the best.

People went to these picnics by horse transportation of course, some riding and others driving in diverse conveyances; probably the most fun was for those who rode in the old bus which used to meet the trains for The Homestead. It is hard to describe this to one who has never seen such a contraption; it had an elongated body, something like a lumber truck, on which were mounted longitudinally rather meagerly upholstered benches, facing inwards, with a canopy over all and the driver in a high seat in front. For these occasions four horses were used instead of the two for the usual train service. The capacity was really about twenty-six but nearer thirty would be squeezed in. There were a number of talented young people who could sing, draw and do sundry parlor tricks, and the hour or two drive was generally uproarious. Of course, if serious courting was in order a runabout and one horse was more suitable, or a couple of horses to ride.

Sometimes, in addition to the dowagers in surreys, there were more elaborate equipages, as when Cole Scott brought his four-in-hand while courting lovely Hildreth Dunn. George Ingalls, who really knew how to drive, often took the family break, which held eight and was drawn by a "spike" team—that is two horses abreast and one in the lead.    That, incidentally, is quite an efficient hitch in mountainous country, with narrow and not too smooth roads, but it takes some driving if you have anything other than farm horses.

Even when there was no objective, such as a picnic or a visit to the White, Nimrod Hall or the like, long trips with a horse were distinctive of life at Hot Springs on through the first decade of the twentieth century before the motor car debauched the love of venturing up lonesome hollows and over rocky hillsides, substituting therefor the thrill of speed and the glamour of distance.  People took these long rides usually in parties of from four to six, with one or more of the group familiar with the terrain or able to follow a trail unmarked by beaten track, spotting ancient blaze marks on the trees.

My mother particularly loved these informal drives. Her daily jaunts were routine and, just to be prepared, she never went without a well-stocked picnic basket.  At lunch she would announce where she was going and more often than not those youngsters who rode would arrange their route by trails to wind up around tea time at some spot by the side of a stream, to find tea, sandwiches and cookies waiting.  Occasionally, instead of riding, I would ask a girl to drive. My sister, Abbie, and her friend, Sally Colston, were ubiquitous and if they heard I was driving, begged to go along.  Perhaps I was not anxious for the company of two youngsters but it was hard to refuse them.  A bit of diplomacy solved the problem.  I would drive the family break, which had two dos-a-dos seats and the tailboard, when let down, made a footrest for the rear facing seat.  I convinced the girls that it would be great fun to ride the tailboard with their legs dangling down. Then we played a sort of game; the seat on the tailboard was none too secure and the trick was to get in the middle of a ford and hit a rock or startle the horses so the girls would be left sitting in air until they hit the water. We were all young enough so it was hilarious fun, with no thought of danger, and the conversation on the front seat could be as confidential as wished. While these drives went everywhere the favorite meeting spot for tea was at the entrance to the Richardson gorge of the Jackson, now called the Jungles from the riot of laurel and rhododendron. There were many different trails leading to this point, about seven miles, just a good distance. The spot is now on Folly Farm, owned by the Hirshes.

The trails of Bath and Highland Counties have existed from time immemorial and are innumerable. In the beginning these were game trails; that the buffalo were not too remote is indicated by the names of the Cowpasture, Bullpasture and Calf Pasture Rivers, so called by the early settlers from the animals found along their banks. Then the Indians used the trails and after that the settlers. Most of them paid little attention to grades, although some of the oldest evidenced remarkable adroitness in getting from here to there. They went from where a stream or "gorge" could be crossed to a point where a rocky ridge was passable, but in between as straight as possible. When highways were built they seldom followed the old trails although these were often heavily used long after roads came. For example, there is a trail, or was twenty years ago, which started at a ford over the Jackson on McKee Dunn's river farm, crossed Back Creek Mountain, to descend on the other side to Back Creek. Long after the highway was built to Mountain Grove cattle were driven over the trail, saving some five or six miles. It was a full day's expedition to go over this trail, returning by road, with a stop on Back Creek for a sandwich and to rest the horses. It was lovely—climbing Back Creek Mountain, first through a grove of oaks; in early spring there was a riot of color under these trees from the wild lupine and yellow azalea. They probably still bloom but who today is willing to ride a horse all day, the last ten miles home over a hard road, just for a few wild flowers?

Another lovely long trail ride was up the Delafield Road, across the ridge and over Big Brushy Mountain down into the Deeds Country, then absolute wilderness, and home by Bath Alum. The Deeds Country is still lovely, part of a national forest with a splendid black road through it, but something is missing when you don't have to stop and hunt for old blaze marks to see if you are getting lost.

Civilization now has come to most trails, at least to all that can be ridden out and back in not over four hours. A few follow the ancient routes, such as the Ritchie, which was once the only access to the Sprouse farm where Dr. Torrence now has his home, "Sleepy Hollow." The McDannald is an old trail, although to get better footing the location has been shifted from the hollow to the side of a shale hill. The Lonesome is as it has been for generations, once providing access to the Clarkson farm, now just a name on a surveyor's map and abandoned so long the trees growing on it seem like virgin timber. Coles Hollow and the Winding Trail are old, too, as is the Beulah, a lovely ride but now so seldom used.

You can't improve on nature, it is said, yet it must be admitted that some of the completely artificial trails which have come into being with the change in habits are better than the old; they are not so narrow, there are not so many unexpected pitches and their surface, mostly shale, is easier for both rider and horse. Over many two can ride abreast, which usually, though not always, adds to their charm; such are the Indian Fort, Gabe Hollow, the Open, the Homestead, the Katydid and many more.

It is not only that visitors to the Valley do not care for long rides over primitive trails which has caused a decrease in the number of what might be called indigenous trails. (Incidentally, be it noted that in the nineties anyone who spoke of a trail would be looked at as trying to be high hat—they were called paths in those days.) There are not now so many farms or places where a trail is necessary for access. Extension of roads and the fact that a few miles more or less makes little difference when using a motor car brought about the abandonment of many. Even more important has been the disappearance of a large proportion of the isolated farms.

# 12. Diversions Along the Road

I T IS uncertain when the first tennis court appeared at The Homestead; one existed as early as 1897, but my recollection of this is for a reason not connected with tennis itself.

After my brother, Albert, graduated from Harvard he spent a year in Germany. Among other things, he brought back a fox terrier named Doch, a smart little dog, not very well trained and with a penchant for getting into trouble. Once Albert took him into a wine shop in Wiesbaden. The bottles were arranged in long rows on a counter running the depth of the store. The proprietor's cat was sitting on the counter at the end nearest the entrance and as they came in the door, Doch saw the cat, jumped on the counter and, running down its entire length, knocked every bottle to one side or the other. The proprietor never caught either Doch or Albert but Albert cut his stay short in Wiesbaden.

Doch was barely tolerated by the rest of the family but Albert attributed all sorts of sterling qualities to the animal, among others, claiming he was the champion of all champions in killing rats.

A war on rats was right up my alley. The livery stable was swarming with rodents and I practised sharp-shooting with a twenty-two. I had heard of rat-killing contests and suggested it would be fun to have one and see just how Doch operated. The idea went over big and Albert said the ideal place for the show would be the tennis court. Some raised the point that if turned loose the rats might get away before Doch could get in his licks but Albert was sure they could not.

The day for the show came. Benches were put about the court and every seat was taken, with many standees. I had a dozen active rats in a wire trap and when all was ready carried my trap out to the center of the court, Albert beside me, with Doch jumping and snapping at the wires of the trap. Albert stood back, holding Doch's collar, while I unlatched the back of the trap and shook the rats out. If I do say it, I had a fine collection, some huge grey granddaddies and some young and full of pep.

When the first rat hit the ground Doch went for him with a snarl. Unfortunately, these were American and not the German rats on which Doch had been trained, and they did not cooperate. One rat fastened on Doch's nose and, with a yelp, he headed for the house. In the meantime the other eleven rats lost no time looking for a place of safety. Bear in mind that all this happened at a time when the gals were not as emancipated as they now are and when they wore more voluminous petticoats and other nether garments. Also legs were considered rather secret if interesting appendages. The benches lined the court on all sides; a rat would head toward these and, seeing the people, turn to look for another exit from the arena. Shrieks rent the air, the girls climbed the benches, upsetting some, and there was such a display of lingerie and underpinnings as The Homestead had never seen. If any scene could be described as bedlam, this deserved the name.

In the course of time the rats all got away and peace returned. With complete injustice, I thought, the blame for the fracas fell on the head of the gangling, fifteen-year-old boy who had furnished the rats instead of on Albert or even Doch, who, after all, was the real cause of the mischief.

The first tennis court was on the lawn in front of the entrance near the present graveled area for horses. There was only one court and no room for another. It must have been shortly after that three courts were put in by the casino in their present location; for some time the upper court was preserved, used mostly by the youngest players. After this tennis began to take a large place in the life at Hot Springs. Undoubtedly, one reason for its popularity was the good fortune which brought outstanding professionals as instructors and general factotums. The first was George Agutter, followed by Jimmie Burns, who soon brought Tobey Hansen in as his assistant. For short times, as assistants or accessories, other pros, such as Mike Dolan, were added but this triumvirate dominated the courts for over fifty years.

My sister, Gladys, was a tennis fan, playing a graceful if not a top game. The first tournaments grew out of the house parties she arranged, built around Marion Fenno, George Wrenn and Bill Larned. These were usually over Labor Day and the tournaments thus started are the direct ancestors of the annual fall tournaments, now usually commencing the last Monday in September. For many years Bill Larned came and played. Though there have been great players since, taking into consideration not only his skill at the game but his sportsmanship, he deserves top ranking.

First and last, pretty nearly every outstanding tennis player for the past fifty years has been seen on the Homestead courts and most of them have played in the spring and fall tournaments. The veteran of them all, still entering the doubles, is Bill Clothier. I think he first came with Norris Williams, who returned many years although missing now for some time. Tilden played as an amateur; Bobbie Riggs won one of the tournaments as an amateur and has returned since as a pro, for exhibition matches. Of the girls, from Marion Fenno and Eleanora Sears down to Kay Stammers and Helen Wills, all have been here and in these tournaments.

Of recent years headline names have not been so frequent. That is probably my fault. In the early days such men as the Wrenns, Larned, Norris Williams and Bill Clothier were truly amateurs but as time went on both men and women began to realize that top tennis had a money value and to cash in on their chance. I am enough of a democrat to respect any man who makes his living doing a job well, whether that be playing mumble putty or running the United States Steel Corporation, and have known many tennis pros for whom I have nothing but admiration. But to pretend that you are playing tennis for fun while at the same time making a good living out of it sub rosa is something else again. If I got anything out of Harvard it was a hatred of hypocrisy and this pseudo amateurism smacks of that.

The thing began in a small way. At first, an attractive man or girl would be invited to play in a tournament, refuse because he or she could not afford the trip, and then someone interested would invite them as a house guest. This went on to where clubs and hotels provided free room and board, laundry and transportation. Theoretically it was only expense money, but that was a sham. Here at Hot Springs we went along with the crowd but two things happened which thoroughly disgusted me. A group of California so-called amateurs, who were touring the tennis circuit, offered to come to Hot Springs if expenses were paid. The players were then at The Greenbrier and I asked what, roughly, the expenses were going to be. I was handed a list with the amount each player said it would cost him. No two amounts were the same but after studying the paper for a time the pattern became clear. The different amounts varied from $25 to $175. The highest figure was what the top-ranking player said it would cost him, the second was the expense for an up-and-coming player, and the balance seemed to vary with attraction to the gallery or reputation as a player. If the payments were just for out-of-pocket expense the thing did not make sense but I fell for the demands. Then, I think it was the fall tournament of the same year, we wanted Bitsy Grant, who had won the tournament before. He asked for transportation from Atlanta to Hot Springs and return. I had the railway people figure out the cost of a ticket, Pullman, meals and an allowance for tips and sent the check along. Grant got here riding in a friend's car but no suggestion of an accounting of the money was ever made.

The tennis tournaments at Hot Springs had always been colorful affairs and there was a tradition of having the top players. The advertising people assured me it was worth as much as the players demanded, or more, to have them and I believe they are right if only financial considerations are taken into account. However, I just could not stomach the business and for the next tournament ruled that any acceptable entrant to the tournament could play, whether staying at The Homestead or elsewhere to save money, but that The Homestead would no longer put up anything in the way of cash or other inducement to bring a tennis player to Hot Springs unless that player was frankly a professional. Perhaps that may seem a pretty rigid rule but with the situation as it developed I could not and cannot see any way to go part way. This policy pretty well shuts out the top players. The gallery may be disappointed if they cannot see Kramer and other stars but the players in the tournament, for which, after all, it is run, probably will be better pleased if they feel they will not run up against a man or woman paid to beat them. Elimination of paid players does not mean necessarily second rate tennis. For the last few years the Reindell and Martin brothers have given us matches well worth watching. If the players are evenly matched and keen, even Class B tennis is fun to watch and all the more so if you know the contestants, which is apt to be the case on the Homestead courts.

Strangely enough, in contrast with tennis, there has never been a demand from a golfer for compensation in return for playing in our tournaments. There have been all sorts, too, even some who slept in their cars because they could not afford a room in a boarding house, and all were welcome if good sportsmen.

Dancing, inherited with other traditions of the Virginia Springs, was always important in the Valley. It is disappointing that I cannot recall the name of the kindly old gentleman who used to arrange for the orchestra to start playing earlier than the regular schedule so the youngsters, whose deadline was ten o'clock by order of stern parents, could have their fun.

For many years there was an extraordinary dancing instructor at The Homestead; I am not going to say that he was the most efficient in the world although many found him a good teacher. He was doing business at White Sulphur when we lived at Grant's Farm and at an early age I was exposed to his instruction. It was always a struggle to think up excuses why I should not have to dress up in stiff clothes and go in for the lesson, sitting dignifiedly beside a driver instead of astride my pony as usual. This man came to Hot Springs later and continued to struggle with my Terpsichorean instruction but if judged by the product he turned out, he could not have been tops in his profession. I wonder now what his nationality was. His name was Laube, which I suppose is German, but he looked and talked less like a German than anyone I have ever known. He was one of the old school, teaching with the most elaborate waving gestures of the arms and hands and wasting interminable time trying to make the boys and girls walk about the ballroom carefully seeing that their toes touched the floor before their heels. He was not entirely concerned with pirouettes and it was under him that the great institution of a Virginia Reel to finish the evening's dancing was in-

augurated. Every Saturday and Wednesday and often
on other nights this was announced loudly by the orchestra
leader when the last dance was through. These reels
were romps in which both young and old joined and
were a wonderful scheme for producing informality and
acquaintanceship.

The Virginia Reels stopped sometime after the east
wing was built. That rather cramped the style of the
ballroom anyway, just as it did the twilight hour on the
casino lawn. Before it was put up there was a wide porch
running entirely around the ballroom except at the
entrance from the lobby. Never was there a finer milieu
for sitting out dances; I hope some who read this will
remember sitting there with chair tilted back against the
rail of the porch, watching a summer moon over the
mountains. Even the most enthusiastic dancer enjoyed
looking through the huge windows at the weaving
couples and listening to a few numbers from the outside.

But to get back to Laube. If dancing was his profession, his avocation was fly fishing. There I struck a
kindred spirit. Laube's technique certainly would not be
considered orthodox today and probably was not then
but he could cast a fly with astounding accuracy and to
great distances. He did it gracefully as well—the flourishes
of his ballroom manner were not apparent; either he left
them out or they simply became a part of a beautifully
rhythmic performance. I am not sure that Laube cared
as much for the actual fishing as he did for casting. We
often went fishing together but between times he would
make me practice casting, and I spent many a long hour
flicking a line about the lawn with a hookless fly on the
end. He was a perfectionist and if in an unguarded
moment I spoke of a "pole" I had to undergo a long

lecture to impress the fact that one fly-fished with a "rod," the pole was reserved for the lowly bait fishermen.

These fishing trips had much beside the actual fishing to recommend them to me. Laube had learned the Greenbrier River when he was at White Sulphur and liked the water from Alderson down. Those were the days of more informal railroading than today. We would take the early morning train from Hot Springs to Covington and then hop the first westbound freight. I used my perquisites, as son of the president of the road, to the uttermost and usually chose the locomotive cab to ride in. A locomotive even today, with automatic stokers and cut and dried instructions to the engineer, is a thing of romance and it was even more so when I was a boy. When it was time to come home we would get a train to Covington and then the night train back to Hot Springs, arriving tired and happy, with more or less fish. We never caught many; I brought home many more when Uncle Louie Cowardin later tried to initiate me into the mysteries of bait fishing but even then I would desert him to go wandering up and down the river following my first love, casting.

Laube took me on many trips and never on any of these was a thing done or a word said which was not suitable for a young boy. I learned later that he was accustomed to drink heavily but, although I was old enough to know what this meant, I never saw evidence of it. I said above that I believed he cared more for casting than for fishing and his end confirmed this opinion. Laube went completely crazy and had to be confined to a padded room. He could be quieted, however, if they let him have a rod, even just the butt piece, which he would wave back and forth, going through all the motions of retrieving, making the back cast and then carefully flicking out the imaginary fly to land in an imaginary pool. He died doing this and perhaps that is about as good a way as any for a fisherman to go.

The ballroom, as well as being the home of waltzes and Virginia reels, was the setting for cakewalks, of which there were always a number during the year. Cakewalks continued their popularity long into the twenties but after the early years of the century they were but pale reflections of past glory. Originally they were amateur affairs and completely unsophisticated, with the performers drawn from the waiters and maids in the hotel. The performers enjoyed the show as much as the audience and many had real entertainment talent. The shows were contests, with plenty of hard feeling among the contestants if they did not agree with the decision of the judges, always the most distinguished visitors present.

Inevitably commercialism crept in and the hat was passed; the size of the "take" became the most important part of the occasion for the contestants. Entrepreneurs developed among the colored population and performers were imported. When the purse was divided a policeman had to be present but even he did not always assure orderly distribution. Perhaps at the end, which came in the thirties, the actual performance was technically better than in the old days but then a better show could be seen any day among the Broadway night clubs. The cruder, amateur events, brimming with *joie de vivre*, had something which once gone could never be replaced.

Three or four times a year the ballroom would go completely formal, with Germans, as cotillions were called, elaborately staged. For these there were favors, never extravagant but bright and colorful. The ambition of every cotillion leader was to devise more new and elaborate figures than his predecessors. If he could carry these off and at the same time keep his regimented dancers full of enthusiasm he was a real leader. They were only in the evening, however, for the morning Germans which held such a vogue at White Sulphur, the Warm and the Old Sweet, never became established at the Hot. The young people were too much engrossed in out-of-door life to have much interest in the rather exotic pastime of dancing by daylight.

The life was simple from a modern point of view, with picnics, golf, tennis and riding during the day, then dancing, and, after the music stopped, often a watermelon or Welsh rarebit party, frequently at Ingallscote. Those were the easy days and I seem to remember my mother's chief worry was whether or not, with the guests one or another of the family would bring in, she would be able to avoid thirteen for lunch—fourteen or twelve made no difference but many a time I ate my lunch on the porch in consequence of the taboo.

The years of the first and second decades of the twentieth century were the heyday of the Japanese Room. Old Shep presided and furnished his own "band" which played every night, taking up a collection for their pay. It was "hot" music and one number always brought riotous applause. Whenever a distinguished guest, and the more pompous and formal the better, came to The Homestead he was sure to be asked to a party in the Japanese Room. Then when things got going well it was suggested that he should be shaved to music. One of Shep's troupe would seat the victim in a chair, drape him with the conventional towel and, using a pair of "bones" in each hand, to the accompaniment of the rest of the band, go through all the exaggerated gestures of a fancy

barber, doing a double shuffle and breakdown in the
process. It was quite elaborate, with the "bones" serving
as razor, brush and comb; the stropping of the "bones"
was particularly effective and rhythmical. At the finish
the towel was whisked away to the accompaniment of a
couplet to the effect that the barber must have his tip.

The broker's office in the hotel was a popular
meeting place in the twenties; in the morning every chair
would be taken. The brokers paid The Homestead
$12,000 a year for the office and pressure was always
being brought from other firms for the concession. Today
there is no broker's office and to have one would mean
subsidizing the outfit.

In April and October it seemed as if the New York
Stock Exchange would have to close, so many of the
members and their wives were at Hot Springs. They were
a happy lot and if not carefree, at least sought escape
from the tension of buying and selling, which resulted in
the same thing—a great desire to have a good time.
For ten years these men dominated the spring and fall
life at Hot Springs and when the holocaust at the end of
the era swept them away it left a hole which was not
filled for many years.

The accelerated pace of living, typical of the twenties,
was not so marked along the Road as elsewhere but we
in the Valley did not entirely escape. The passion for
gambling during that hectic era came to Hot Springs;
most of it was across the bridge table and, while generally never wild, there were plenty of rubbers where
the pay-off ran into thousands of dollars. On the golf
courses, also, there were foursomes with large sums
depending on the result. However, all the gambling
at The Homestead was strictly amateur; every after-

noon the Garden Room, then called the Zodiac Room, would have half a dozen tables of bridge. Old Man Ward was the bridge instructor, a true New Englander who had strayed south. He played his cards as well as any of the modern masters and joined in all the games but only for small stakes. The most constant of these players was General Seligman, a kindly, gentle old man, who lost pretty regularly but always with perfect good humor.

It was inevitable that professional gamblers would try to break into the Valley. It was traditional to have a casino at European spas and there were gambling houses at French Lick and White Sulphur. With Fred Sterry managing the Poinciana and The Homestead, many of the guests who went to both places frequented Bradley's in Palm Beach, which was in its heyday. In Hot Springs the gambling war which kept the professionals out went on concurrently with that over the automobile and was not finally settled until 1916. Unlike the automobile conflict, it ended with the capitulation of the gamblers, on terms, however, which made the victory somewhat of a pyrrhic one as it involved buying out the gamblers at a huge price.

The opening gun in this war came in 1910 when Thomas O'Brien purchased the two lots on which Woodland House, now owned by Major W. D. Campbell, stands and announced his intention of opening a casino with all the "fixin's." So far as I ever heard, O'Brien was a pretty decent sort of chap, who wanted to live up to the code of ethics of high class operators of such institutions. Perhaps if he had chosen a more remote location for his activities there might have been less trouble, but to have him right at the front door could not be tolerated since The Homestead was developing as a family resort, not only for the summer season but a place where parents could bring their children during spring vacations.

Life along the Road was gay and carefree, as can be imagined from an adventure during my college years. This is a story which for many years I feared to tell but can "take it" now. That spring I had a succession of attacks of tonsillitis, culminating in a severe quinsy. When this was reported to the college office someone probably remembered that I had almost died a few years before from neglect of a case of appendicitis, and the advice of the doctor that I be given leave of absence for a few weeks in a better climate was accepted. My parents were then in Europe but my brother, George, was at Hot Springs and suggested that I come down with him. I did so, but before I was to return to Cambridge George had to leave. Thinking I was pretty young to be turned loose in the spring life of The Homestead, George asked his good friend, Livy Beeckman, of Newport and New York, to take me under his wing. Perhaps the shelter of that particular wing was more dangerous than exposure to the other elements but it resulted in my having a good time.

Livy and I had a table close to the entrance of the dining room. George had been gone a few days when two gorgeous girls arrived. Of course, they caught Livy's eye and when some of his friends stopped by our table there was a bit of badinage. Someone suggested that it might be difficult to meet the girls but Livy bet twenty-five dollars and champagne for the crowd that he and I would dine with them the next night. I took my share of the bet and wondered how we were going to get out of it.

Ping-pong was then the rage. As we walked out of the dining room, Livy said we ought to have a tournament the next day. "The tournament should have mixed doubles," he said, "and I don't believe those girls know anyone for partners. Anyway, we can spring it quickly enough so no one else can get there first and will ask them to play with us."

It worked. The tournament was held after dinner, Livy playing with one of the girls and I with the other. What more natural than that we four should dine together, as we did. I wish I could remember more of these girls; mine was the best ping-pong player and Livy's the best looker but other than that they were just a pair of nice girls.

In the finals my partner and I were beaten. However, we had to celebrate and Livy had a big party to drink the champagne we had won. The party lasted pretty late and when it broke up my troubles came.

To explain a bit, the hotel was terribly crowded and when George left there wasn't a single room for me. It was early March, however, and a cottage being vacant, they put me in that. I was feeling pretty happy when the party broke up and I went down to my cottage. Anyone familiar with these knows they are much alike. I went up onto the entrance porch of what I thought was my cottage and tried the door, finding it locked. That didn't surprise me as, while I hardly ever locked the door, once in a while the maid who turned down the bed would do so. I always left the window up in my bedroom so walked around the porch, pushed the sash higher and, feeling very happy, instead of climbing in just dove through the window onto the bed. The bed was there as I expected, but on top of it was a female figure which came to life violently and suddenly as I landed. I hope I may never hear another woman's scream such as rent the air. I literally fell out of the window, realizing in a flash that I had the wrong cottage. I ran to the right one and, finding the door unlocked, rushed in and got into bed without turning on the light. I heard a lot of commotion and running around and, panic stricken, waited for someone to knock on my door, which fortunately no one did.

The next morning, on going up to the hotel, I found great excitement and, with discretion, tried to find out what was going on. I learned that a terrible event had taken place. A stout, elderly woman, unable to get a room in the hotel proper, had, much to her regret, taken one in a cottage. She reported that during the night she had been brutally attacked and only presence of mind had saved her virtue. That was pretty bad, but I listened to the rest of the tale. "They will certainly catch the man. The woman got a good look at him and can recognize him anywhere. He was a little, short negro, fat and dumpy, and did not have a coat on." I blessed the lady's imagination. I had never seen her and wanted desperately to do so but was afraid to take chances and kept in the distance if I thought she was coming along.

There was a great hullabaloo and a lot of innocent negroes, who had been seen in the neighborhood, had difficulty accounting for their whereabouts that night. Of course the mystery was not solved and for more than twenty years I never told even my best friend what happened to me that night. It was the end of a perfect day but in the course of the next I decided it was best to get back to my studies.

## 13. The Great Travel the Road

MANY Presidents of the United States have visited the Valley. Of course, Thomas Jefferson did, but careful research has failed to discover any record of a presidential visit between his and that of President William McKinley. McKinley made a considerable stay but my personal recollections of this are most fragmentary. It is hard to understand why this is so. In 1896, when competing with John R. McLean for the leadership of the Democratic Party in Southern Ohio, my father could not swallow Free Silver and bolted the party, coming out "whole hog" for McKinley. He had bitter words with Mark Hanna over the policies of the campaign in the Middle West, Hanna wanting first of all to win that particular election and my father wanting to build for the future with a campaign of education. In spite of the disagreement with Hanna over policies in conducting the campaign, father was a factor in the election and cordial relations always existed between the President and him. In consequence, when McKinley was at Hot Springs he and my father had many talks but, though often present at these, I gained no lasting impressions. Perhaps, after all, McKinley was a rather negative character which did not impress even a boy in his late teens, already somewhat of an iconoclast.

I do remember, however, McKinley's gentleness and courtesy toward Mrs. McKinley, then a complete invalid. He used to drive with her every afternoon. A fine pair of horses meant much in those days and there was friendly rivalry among residents to provide the best team for these events. Dr. Brandt was a lover and owner of fine horses and his team was usually designated although Fred Sterry and a local liveryman, Jimmie Hamilton, were close seconds.

President Taft came to the Hot often both before and after he became President. When we lived in Cincinnati the Tafts had a house nearby. My father and Mr. Taft used to meet at our driveway and walk part way into town every morning. I usually traipsed along, as I had two miles to go to school and for half the distance my route coincided with theirs. Mr. Taft was then a United States District Judge and to a young boy he was what he ever remained, a very fine gentleman.

Years later, after my father became enmeshed in Hot Springs, he used to have stag parties at Thanksgiving to which Mr. Taft was always invited and to many of which he came. I remember one of these about 1902. While not directly connected with the Valley, the trip was the occasion of one of the most illuminating experiences of my life with a truly great man. Of course it was against all rules to be absent from college classes immediately before or after a holiday and yet I had to be if I were to join the party, which I was desperately anxious to do. I didn't dare take a chance and just go off, so took my courage in both hands and went to see Dean Briggs. I got a preemptory refusal right at the start. I kept at him and asked that he look at my record. He did and, with his gentle smile, remarked, "You have already had a good many absences, Mr. Ingalls."

There was no denying the truth of that statement but I insisted my marks were always satisfactory and that I had never been in any trouble. Briggs studied the record in silence and then said, "We must have inflexible rules." A long pause—"The best thing about inflexible rules is that they can be broken with discrimination." I was flabbergasted and asked if that meant I might go. "Oh, no. I was not talking about your going off."

I looked at him for what seemed an uncomfortable hour and then left, wondering what I should do. In the end I went and never heard anything from the Dean's office about the cuts I took. There may have been educators more capable of handling adolescents than Briggs but, if so, I have never met one. It was not only what he did for me, but his whole manner and understanding of the boy before him, which I could not help feeling. Unfortunately, it never became my privilege to know Briggs beyond formal lines, but from that time on I would have cut off my right hand rather than let him down.

This was a wonderful house party. Mr. Taft was one of the guests. My brother, Ed, was another and, with him, Tom Slocum, whom any Harvard man between the classes of '90 and his death in 1937 will remember as having the biggest heart and most entertaining personality of them all. Colonel Colston was another. Joe Wilby and Judge J. W. Warrington, of Cincinnati, were along, and Jacob Schmidlapp, then the leading banker in that city. There were others whose names escape me. We had a break in the weather, always chancy in the Valley at Thanksgiving time, and there was golf, mostly of a weird variety—in general, the more brilliant the guests the worse their golf. But the conversation was more valuable as education than anything a young man could possibly have gained from any number of college lectures.

Mr. Taft returned to Hot Springs from time to time after he was President.

Our next Presidential visitor was Woodrow Wilson, who came for part of his honeymoon when he married Mrs. Edith Bolling Galt. At that time I was living in New York and was not in the Valley while he was here. I find that few have any recollection of his visit other than that it naturally created a lot of interest. Aloof and formal in any event, he always avoided publicity and particularly on this occasion. The couple drove frequently but spent most of the time while here in their suite.

President Coolidge also came to The Homestead with Mrs. Coolidge, and this time I was at Hot Springs. While as a rule I prefer bird shooting to lion hunting, I had an immense desire to meet Calvin Coolidge and talk with him. I don't know whether my feeling was admiration or curiosity but it was real none the less. For

some reason or other no good opportunity presented itself until one evening Coolidge was coming up from the
movies and someone introduced me to him. His greeting
was rather on the short side and having finished the conventional polite remarks he turned to Mrs. Coolidge and
said, "Where did you put my soda bi-carb? I want it
*now*." He marched away and I felt that my mental
pigeonhole for him was well and satisfactorily filled.

Herbert Hoover spent some time at The Homestead
in 1929 and later on was a speaker at a meeting which
was held here. George Warrington, my brother-in-law,
who was living in his cottage, Edgewood, had been one
of Hoover's chief assistants when he was Food Adminis-
trator during the first World War. They became close
friends and it was through this association that I saw
quite a bit of Hoover during his first visit.

Later on Franklin Roosevelt made his only visit to
Hot Springs. He was Governor of New York and had
been asked to be a speaker at one of the summer conferences at the University of Virginia. I had known him
rather well in college and also knew how hot Charlottes-
ville can be in July, when this affair was going on, so I
asked him to spend Saturday and Sunday with me. He
came to our house, The Yard, but I had never realized
before that almost every room in the house is at a different
level. Personally I think that rather attractive, but
after we got Franklin in the house it was apparent it was
going to be pretty difficult taking care of him. I telephoned
the hotel and got him a suite next to an elevator. Judge
William Clark, who had been in Roosevelt's club in
Harvard, was living at Hot Springs and that evening we
all had dinner together and sat around afterwards. About
ten o'clock I roused the attendant at the pool and we had a
swim, then came back to Roosevelt's rooms for a drink

and further talk. It so happened that, although I saw him frequently, this was the only occasion after he became a national figure when we had a chance for an informal talk. Unfortunately, Morgenthau was with him. Roosevelt expatiated on every problem the world was facing and oozed pleasure from every pore when Morgenthau marveled at his omniscience.

Once again Roosevelt came in contact with The Homestead. In 1934 the Associated Harvard Clubs were to meet at Hot Springs. Dr. Moore, of St. Louis, was president of the Clubs and, to my dismay, appointed me on a committee to get the President to come to the meeting. James Bryant Conant had just become President of Harvard and this was to be his first opportunity to address the body of the Alumni. We arranged for a meeting at the White House, to extend the invitation. That was in the days of prohibition and I recall that Joe Choate, then prohibition director, was one of the committee to wait on the President. Our reception was cordial and pleasant. We got a promise that he would either be present or would address the Clubs by phone. As we were leaving Roosevelt turned to me and said, "Fay, be sure the boys have plenty of liquid refreshment. I'm glad you have Joe on the committee. He should be able to see that it is all right."

It was not long after that Marvin McIntyre called me by phone and said the President could not be at the meeting. He told me, however, that Roosevelt was anxious to address the Clubs and asked me to be sure to have the wires cleared and good facilities for an hour's speech, starting at noon. I had only $150 from the Virginia Club to make the necessary arrangements and soon found it was going to be a mighty expensive business. Some loyal Harvard men in the A. T. & T. came to the rescue and all was arranged. Conant began his speech about 11:30. At 11:45 one of the A. T. & T. engineers whispered to me that we would have to interrupt Conant for the White House, so I spoke to Moore and Conant, who with good grace withdrew temporarily. There was a tangible silence and then from the loud-speaker, "This is the White House. The next voice you will hear will be that of the President of the United States." I have not the best of memories but can recall every word of Roosevelt's speech. It was as follows:

"I am delighted to congratulate President Conant. We presidents must stand together."

There ensued a tense silence. At last a voice came over saying the President had left the microphone, and it was all over. The proceeding certainly did nothing to reduce the number of economic Tories among the most prominent graduates of the President's Alma Mater.

Convenient as Hot Springs is to the Capital, there was always a large colony of prominent Washingtonians at The Homestead or in the Valley, staying at private houses. Often there would be found some of the staff of the British Embassy, and the French, German and Italian Ambassadors made visits. In our own government practically everyone of prominence came sooner or later. Harry S. Truman, when a member of the Senate with no indication of his future prominence, was one of these and Henry Wallace another.

In view of what happened later, the experience with Hirosi Saito, the Japanese Ambassador, who rented Woodland House, the old gambling place, one summer, is amusing. Saito liked to play golf but hated to pay his green fees. In the late afternoon the embassy car would be found parked by the old toll house near the eighth hole and the Ambassador would be seen knocking a ball around, with his chauffeur as caddy. In view of his diplomatic position the cashier at the club house just winked at the subterfuge.

When Saito came to leave there was an immense bill for sundry luxuries, particularly champagne. A most polite attache called on me and asked if I would not be willing to have this bill rendered in a rather unconventional manner. He said the Japanese Government was to pay for the rent of the house and incidentals thereto out of general funds. However, the Ambassador had exhausted his entertainment allowance and would be embarrassed financially if he had to pay out of his personal funds for the champagne, etc. The attache suggested that of course part of the expense of renting the house was going to be putting it in order and cleaning on departure. Therefore, he asked that the bill be made out for rent so much, then cleaning and incidentals so much, including in the latter item the champagne. It did not seem to be my business if he gypped his government so the bill was rendered, and duly paid, as the attache requested. I often wondered what the Japanese auditors thought of the American way of living, when it became necessary to spend about $1,800 for cleaning women's time after a residence of less than four months.

Frequent visitors to Hot Springs were Senator and Mrs. Chauncey Depew of New York. It was to be expected that Mr. Depew would be popular with those who met him socially but perhaps it was not so well known that his charm was felt by all who came into contact with him. Depew liked to make speeches. I heard him many times, both as an after-dinner speaker and as a campaign orator, but never gave him full credit for his talent until he came to Hot Springs. The Senator usually arrived at the end of June and stayed through July. That put him here over the Fourth. Even then the old-fashioned July Fourth celebration, with flamboyant oratory, was on the wane but it was felt that some sort of official cognizance ought to be taken. It had not yet become an opportunity for auto picnics or watching double-header ball games.

The Senator was much interested in these occasions and always volunteered his services as speaker. They were good speeches, not in the least tawdry or demagogic, but the talk of an educated man who felt deeply the importance of the day; they were effective with his hearers, not only guests of The Homestead but local people whose politics were quite different from the Senator's. He wanted to talk to the "man in the street" and at first did not want to speak in The Homestead theatre, fearing that the local citizenry would not want to come to the hotel. Later, as people came to know him, he spoke in the theatre and there was never any question of his having a full and attentive audience. The Senator had known my father, and always requested that I introduce him to the crowd. I can't say that I enjoyed the task but am sure no one ever accused me of the hideous crime of verbosity in these introductions—I, at least, made a record for brevity.

One of these occasions made trouble for me. The qualifying round of the Virginia State Amateur Golf Tournament was being played on July Fourth. I got an early starting time and thought there would be no question about finishing by noon, when the ceremonies were to begin. The course was crowded and play slower and slower. I got to the seventeenth hole with time left to just squeak through. Then the pair before us got into trouble and I grew more and more nervous. I had par on the last two holes for something better than eighty, which would qualify easily, but, thinking of what would happen if I kept the Senator and audience waiting, I was more and more jittery and managed to do everything a golfer should not on the seventeenth hole, ending up with a twelve and, picking my ball off the green, hurried away without playing the eighteenth hole.

One of these golf tournaments a year or so later gave the Senator an opportunity for a speech, which I believe was the gem of all such in my experience. In those days quite a feature was made of the presentation of prizes for the tournament and the Golf Association always tried to get some distinguished man to hand them out. The Senator was asked to officiate and consented, though saying he did not know much about golf. There was a large gathering, not only for the event but because people wanted to hear the Senator speak. The first trophy to be presented was the medal for low qualifying score. The President of the Golf Association handed this to the Senator, at the same time telling him who won it and saying the prize was for the lowest score in the qualifying round. I was sitting near the rostrum and saw that the Senator looked puzzled. As I recall the speech it was about as follows:

"Ladies and gentlemen, I have been asked to present the prizes for this most important event and am delighted to do so. I told your President that I was not familiar with the game of golf but that any sporting competition was always close to my heart. I really have wondered at the hold the game of golf is gaining on Americans but it was not until this moment that I realized what this game has which others do not. In most games the prize is awarded to the best player, the one who accomplishes the most. I see that with golf it is different. Here I am about to award the first and most important prize to the man who made the lowest score, in other words, to

absolutely the worst player. It is obvious that the re-
wards in golf do not go to the most skillful performer but
to the most diligent and earnest, laboring under the
greatest difficulties. Mr. Doe, I am delighted to present
this trophy to you, marking you as the best sportsman if
not the most skillful player in the tournament."

For a few minutes the audience was confused. Was
the Senator just being facetious? A few murmured that
it was discourteous to treat so lightly the winning of a
major trophy, but the Senator's question to the President,
who was holding the next trophy, was overheard, which
was to please explain when there was an opportunity
why the booby prize was given first. As the purport of
the question sank home the audience went into hysterics.
Only a man of the Senator's long experience in public
appearances could have retained his dignity as did Depew
in the face of the demonstration, though the reason for
it was completely blind to him. However, waiting until
the noise died down, the Senator proceeded with the
presentation of the remaining trophies, each with a
graceful little speech. But he knew something was
wrong and in the few words to each of the winners
carefully avoided any mention of the game of golf.

## *14. Dynastic Changes*

SINCE that summer of 1888 when M. E. Ingalls conducted his syndicate through the Valley, the
Ingalls family has played a major part in the life
along the Road. While the family as a unit has had its
influence, three particular members have at different
periods been leading factors, M. E. Ingalls from 1889 to
1914, M. E. Ingalls, Jr., from 1914 to 1922, and the writer
of this volume from 1922 on. The successions never interrupted the pattern of life in the Valley but each came
under conditions which strained the fabric.

Although dominating the scene more completely than either of his sons, M. E. Ingalls never held office in the Virginia Hot Springs Company, never knew much about the mechanical operation of the hotel and never technically owned a majority of the stock of the Company; he nevertheless had a deep love for the Valley and made it his real home. By his immense driving power, an appalling ability to assimilate details and the gift of inspiring loyalty in those who worked for him, he directed affairs at Hot Springs as a czar. In 1913 he had a stroke and it was plain that the end was not far off. At that time he was president of a large bank in Cincinnati, Chairman of the Board of the Big Four Railway, and everything at Hot Springs. Something had to be done, not only for these interests but many others and my three brothers, Ed, George and Albert, and I had a long and sorrowful conference. We got father to resign from the railroad, and Mr. Lee Ault, of Cincinnati, an old friend, agreed to take over the bank.

Then something had to be done about Hot Springs. Ed Ingalls had a well established law practice, George and Albert were top executives in the New York Central, and my law practice was just becoming profitable. None of us knew anything about a hotel, the core of Hot Springs. Yet even our minority interest represented a good deal of money, we had a home here and all loved the place.

At last Ed found the solution. The largest interest in the original syndicate was that held by J. P. Morgan and Company. When the elder Morgan sold the Chesapeake and Ohio for the syndicate, to Cassatt of the Pennsylvania, he forgot that it also owned Hot Springs and a lot of other things. Cassatt was only interested in the railroad and, in a stormy interview, Morgan told my father he had given his word to Cassatt that he would sell the railway alone and said my father would just have to work out the balance of the syndicate's holdings. It took years of litigation to clear up other matters, such as steamship lines, and Hot Springs just drifted along. In the course of time the bitterness between my father and Morgan was forgotten and friendly relations re-established. J. P. Morgan, Jr., had been a few years before Ed in college and was a close friend of Tom Slocum, with whom Ed lived for so many years in New York. Ed suggested that if the Morgan firm would sell to us their investment in Hot Springs, we could then control the property and have a sufficient stake to justify one of us making it his prime interest. Ed thought he could hold his existing legal connections and still give the major part of his attention to Hot Springs, and that was the way it worked out. If the elder Morgan had been rough in 1899, the younger made amends in 1914 and we bought the control of the Company at a price which represented only the original cost and interest although the property had greatly increased in value.

When Ed Ingalls came to Hot Springs he found things at loose ends. Due to ill health my father's control had slipped for several years and the only bright spot in the picture was a sizable reserve in gilt-edge securities for the Company. Fred Sterry, still nominally manager, was deeply absorbed in Florida and the Plaza, and The Homestead had been neglected. It was shabby and run-down in every department. Sterry left pretty nearly everything to an assistant manager, McLaughlin—Mac, as everyone knew him, an Irishman who must have been born under the shadow of the Blarney Stone; I think he could have sold Brooklyn Bridge to Russell Sage and, what is more, after the storm blew over, had a friend for life. Mac always promised anyone everything but, while he seemed to get away with it, the glamour was fading.

The first thing Ed did was to install a new manager, Henry Albert, who was a competent man and soon brought order out of chaos. Unfortunately, Albert, in the vernacular, was "behind the eight ball" from the start. In the first place, he was a German and very German at that. With the outbreak of the war he was suspect on all sides. There were also flaws in the organization with which he was unable to cope. In 1917 he resigned and was succeeded by Christian Andersen, who continued as manager until his death in 1931.

The elimination of European travel brought more business than could be handled and Andersen was a strong and capable manager. His sterling honesty and fairness instilled confidence and loyalty in the employees. When first appointed, Ed was criticised for picking another foreigner, for Andersen was a Dane, but the outcome showed clearly enough it was the man who counted, not where he came from.

Ed found a problem which still plagues the hotel industry, that is that it takes an ever-increasing amount of sleeping space to take care of the same number of people. The Homestead was unbalanced as between public rooms and sleeping quarters, so Ed conceived the idea of an addition. This materialized in the east wing. The architects were again Elzner and Anderson but unfortunately the job of building was let to the lowest bidder, a nationally known contractor. The job was probably too small for such a large organization and out of its line anyway. The result was much shoddy workmanship, the poorest ever done at Hot Springs and still a headache to the maintenance people.

Some years later Ed decided there should be an a la carte dining room and theatre. The addition housing the Garden Room, ballroom, Empire Room and theatre was therefore built, completed in 1921. As the entrance road from the station then ran across what is now the formal garden it had to be changed. My mother's guiding hand for planting was gone and Mr. Gallagher, a member of the firm of Olmstead Brothers, of Boston, was called in to design a new entrance. He laid out the formal garden and for many years thereafter, on semiannual visits, supervised all of the planting about the hotel grounds.

There was now a shuffling of my family's houses. Ed bought Ingallscote, changing the name to Ingallston, and my mother White Cottage, immediately adjacent, originally built by E. F. Osborn, one of my father's associates in the Big Four. Mother lived in the White Cottage until my sister purchased Boxwood Farm. White Cottage, after Mother and Gladys went to Boxwood, remained in the family, and when Ed died his widow sold Ingallston to B. F. Jones, of Pittsburgh, and moved to the White Cottage, living there until her death.

Boxwood Farm, one of the oldest houses in the Valley, was bought by my sister, Gladys, in 1916. I cannot learn when the house was built but about 1825 it was purchased by a Dr. Archer, who owned it until 1850. Archer, a contemporary of Dr. Goode, was one of the first practicing physicians in the Valley. After Archer's death the property passed to the McDannalds, a prominent family in the county. Close to the main house was a little building, altered to make a guest house when Gladys Ingalls acquired the property, which William McDannald and his son, Judge C. R. McDannald, used as a law office. There is an apocryphal story that someone who had worked in this little law office died of diphtheria. When Gladys remodeled the buildings two of the workmen came down with the same disease. The latter is surely true, but the tradition that the germs had lain dormant over many years is open to question.

Gladys built a stable and modernized the main house by putting in plumbing and heating but left the general arrangement and exterior lines exactly as they were. She and mother lived at Boxwood only a short time, for in 1917 Gladys married Malcolm Arnold Robertson, then Secretary of the British Embassy in Washington. Not long after she joined her husband at The Hague, to which post he had been transferred, and Boxwood was sold to the Edgar Parkes.

Edgar had made and lost several fortunes but his financial troubles never upset him. I remember once going up to New York on the train with him. It was a brisk fall day and, having heard a few stories, I guessed that the reason Edgar was not wearing an overcoat was because of the state of the treasury. But he was carrying his cane and traveled in a drawing room, to which he invited me to share some fine old brandy. The Parkes were later divorced but Mrs. Parke and her mother stayed on at Boxwood until they both died.

Boxwood was then bought by Huntington Hartford, who made a few structural alterations, hardly changing it, and installed in it some very fine early American furnishings. The interior is now a gem. When Hartford married he gave Boxwood to his wife for a wedding present and when they were divorced she kept it. She then married Douglas Fairbanks, Jr. They live in the house at times but recently have usually rented it to others.

Until 1913 the life of the residents of the Valley, except such as were employed by the Company, was little changed by all the growth connected with The Homestead. In that year, however, a movement was started which was to have far-reaching effects.

My sister, Gladys, mostly through her riding, had come to know a great many of the local people and the conditions under which they lived, particularly those in out-of-the-way localities. In that year she heard of two distressing cases of illness on isolated farms, one of pellagra and the other of typhoid. Investigating these, Gladys was struck with the lack of knowledge of hygiene and the impossibility of outlying families getting any sort of nursing whatsoever. It occurred to her that the only solution was the establishment of a Visiting Nurse Service. It is not often realized how recent modern rural visiting nurse service is but that will be apparent from the letter written by Miss Mabel Boardman, Chairman of the Executive Committee of the American Red Cross, which was read at a meeting in October, 1913, when a nursing service had been established at Hot Springs for six months on a tentative basis. This letter said she wished to congratulate those who had made the beginning upon "the successful establishment of the first Red Cross Rural Nursing Association in America."

My sister worked indefatigably on the project and its success was really due to her tact and efforts. In the beginning she discussed her plans with Dr. Henry S. Pole, who advised her that first of all she should see Dr. C. M. Thomas, who had by far the largest rural practice. Gladys found Dr. Thomas a fine example of country doctor. He was a skillful physician, also a man with shrewd appreciation of human nature, and wholeheartedly interested in anything which might improve living conditions in the Valley. His assistance was invaluable, not only in assuring the cooperation of other physicians, but by giving his public approval he opened many doors which otherwise would have been closed to Gladys.

An excellent nurse was obtained and an association formed called the Hot Springs Valley Nursing Association. The beginnings were hard. Mrs. Frank Hopkins, with whom Gladys had worked on many charitable projects, assisted and persuaded Thomas A. Sterrett, Jr., to act as treasurer. From the time the Association was formed until his death in 1946 Tom Sterrett continued as treasurer, and during the many vicissitudes of the Association proved an invaluable balance wheel and tireless worker. For all of this he never received a dollar of compensation even for clerical help, although the work was onerous and, not a rich man, his own business made heavy demands on him.

It was not long before the nurse's horse and buggy became a feature of the community. None of the nurses who were employed had included in their training lessons in driving but the horse, "Old Joe," ought to have a monument for he took them anywhere at any time for years, until the day of the horse passed and a motor car took his place. If a car could have been obtained with the intelligence of Old Joe much grief would have been avoided.

It soon became apparent that welfare work and education were as much needed as actual nursing. To be successful this meant breaking down barriers inherent among an isolated but immensely proud population. Very early two hundred members were recruited for the Association, each paying a small fee so no one considered the service a charity. To get people together Gladys conceived the idea of a "Social Supper" where volunteers would provide the food and all the countryside be invited. These suppers were in the beginning camouflaged as a means of raising money but the real purpose was to stir

up enthusiasm. They were immensely successful and
were held annually for many years until conditions,
mostly of transportation, radically changed.

The next step was to get a building for social affairs
and quarters for the visiting nurse. This meant raising
considerable money. Gladys sought contributions in any
amount, however small, and obtained a gratifying re-
sponse. Of course, the Valley could not do the job by
itself and many guests of The Homestead put their
shoulders to the wheel. Mrs. Stuyvesant Fish was one
of the first to organize a committee to help. As a contribution, Henri de Sibour, of Washington, volunteered to make
plans for the building. Mr. and Mrs. Stewart Waller were
most generous, not only while the drive for building funds
was on but thereafter. When Mr. Waller died his widow
gave $10,000 in his memory, the first substantial donation
toward an endowment. The final push over the financial
hill was made by Mr. and Mrs. John D. Rockefeller, Jr.
He was fond of picnics and I think Gladys tried to arrange
that he should see some of the life of the rural people when
she planned these. It was not a case of gold digging, but
she could not help talking about the people who owned
the stream banks on which they ate their lunch. On
July first, 1916, the cornerstone of the building was laid
with proper ceremonies, including a speech by Senator
Burton, of Ohio, and in October of that year the Community House was opened.

Gladys was president of the Association until 1919,
when she went abroad to live. She was then elected
honorary president, which she still is, and on her all too
infrequent visits to this country takes as great an interest
as ever.

With the impetus Gladys gave to the Association it
throve and has since been of increasing value to the com-

munity. The type of service it renders has changed with
the times. When the visiting nurse first began her work,
except for a few farms in the Valley proper it was almost
a day's journey to come to Hot Springs to see a doctor
and visits to social functions or even friends were few
and far between. It is hard to appreciate that as late as
1904 the clay roads (and the Valley Road was only paved
between Warm Springs and Healing Springs) were
frequently impassable for weeks at a time in spring when
the frost was coming out of the ground. It was often impossible to drive over such an important road as that
through Dunn's Gap from early March until late April
except in a farm wagon with a pair of draft horses. Today
even the most remote lanes are always passable and for
years I do not recall having to use chains except when
there is ice. Harry Byrd's getting secondary road maintenance put under an efficient State Highway Department has worked something like a miracle.

With better highways, even the poorest farmers
acquired some sort of jalopy or truck. In consequence they
came to Hot Springs for the movies, to visit friends and
attend church functions. These things all tended to break
down isolation. In the matter of health, it is no longer
necessary to plan weeks ahead for a woman to go to the
Community House for prenatal advice or to have her
children checked over, and in cases of acute illness it is
now possible to take the patient to the hospital.

With these changes the usefulness of the Community
House as a center of social life rapidly disappeared and
at the same time calls on the visiting nurse diminished.
On the other hand its use as a hospital and its facilities,
such as the small but well equipped laboratory and X-
ray room grew apace, more rapidly as the backwoods people became educated to the idea of a hospital. In spite of

the almost constant remodeling which finally took the whole building for a hospital, the Association has not been able to meet the demand. At the moment of writing this, work has begun on further alterations which, if the money holds out, will give the Valley an excellently equipped modern hospital.

Mrs. Edgar Parke succeeded Gladys as head of the Association and did a good job. Then a few years after we came to the Valley my wife was elected president and has since continued in that office.

It is quite probable that ultimately more modern conditions would have permeated to the mountain people even if the Nursing Association had never been formed. However, if one will but drive over back roads some thirty or forty miles from The Homestead one will realize that progress does not come automatically nor always along desirable lines when not wisely directed. Good roads and motor cars would have come in any event but it is doubtful if the transition from the narrow, isolated life of pioneers to that of the modern world would have been accomplished as successfully as it has been without the Association and the spirit with which it was founded and has subsequently been carried on.

Similar responsibilities to those assumed by Gladys have fallen on the next Ingalls generation. Before her marriage our daughter, Polly, spent most of her time at Hot Springs and became much interested in the children of the County, most of whom went to the consolidated schools in the Valley. This consolidation of the schools made it necessary for many of these children to bring luncheons with them. Many families living in the remote districts could not really afford to furnish the proper kind of food and more used poor judgment in what they put up for the children. A

child picked up before dawn at Mountain Grove and
having to ride in a school bus eighteen miles to Hot
Springs, then to return home after dark, needed food with
fuel in it to get through the day and thrive.

Polly determined to do something about this. When
she started her work the idea of luncheons to be provided
by the schools was in its infancy. The thing could not be
handled upon a direct charitable basis, the easiest way,
for many children, probably those who needed them most,
would not have taken the luncheons. Polly went to work
on the parents, organizing committees in each little settlement and getting people to volunteer in all sorts of ways.
The scheme was so successful that when Polly turned to
war work and left the Valley it was going so strong that
public opinion was sufficient to make the school authorities carry on officially.

Again in 1922 there came a change in the head of the
dynasty. In September Ed Ingalls, while in New York,
had an attack of appendicitis. There was no reason to
suppose this was serious, and on the night of the twenty-
first my wife and I were preparing to celebrate a wedding
anniversary at our home on Long Island. We had squeezed
into our wedding clothes, though the cutaway was pretty
tight for me, and were having a lot of fun with the children
when the telephone rang and Ed's Japanese chauffeur told
me I should come up right away if I wanted to see Ed
alive, as something had gone wrong with the operation.
Without changing clothes we drove up to the hospital
but were too late, for Ed was unconscious and died the
next day.

Ed's death threw the responsibility for Hot Springs
back on the three remaining brothers. I was having a
tough time just then. In 1913 I had almost given up my
law practice to be general counsel for a large manu-

facturing company. I went with them first of all to do some simple legal work but almost immediately found myself catapulted into a position in the active management. I was really too young for the responsibility and, what made it worse, the concern was one of the key industries for military preparation. Until the close of the war the pressure of work was terrific. I was pretty well run down at the end but so was everyone else and I didn't think much of my troubles until one day in 1921 when trying to fix the plumbing on a washstand I discovered, to my amazement, that a pipe kept appearing and disappearing. Shifting my head from side to side I found that when the line of sight of my left eye was interfered with I could not see anything—I was blind in my right eye. I had noticed that I could not play golf or shoot as well as previously but up to that moment had no idea one eye was bad.

The next day I hied myself to an oculist and then went through all the gamut of the medicos, trying to find out what had happened. I never did discover, except that possibly I had been put together wrongly when they took me apart after my appendicitis years before, or else had run the machine too hard during the war years. At all events I was told I would be completely blind within two years and that my life expectancy was but a few years; however, if I would give up work and live out-of-doors and sensibly I might do a bit better. Such a verdict is not good for the morale and I was at sixes and sevens what to do.

When George, Albert and I talked over Hot Springs, George made the suggestion that I throw up my job and go down to take charge of things. I demurred at first for I knew nothing about a hotel except what one learns by visiting one once in a while, and didn't feel up to grappling with an entirely new set of problems. I was about as near licked as I have ever been and think I should have folded up had it not been for my wife; she not only gave me courage but assured me she did not mind leaving the place we had built and all the friends we had on Long Island, which I knew was a lie but one so convincingly told that I could not help believe she would be glad to do all that if it would give me a chance. George and Albert said that we all had confidence in Andersen, who was then manager of The Homestead, and they thought if I would go down, act as sort of Chairman of the House Committee, telling Andersen to fix something up if I knew it was wrong even if I did not know why, if I would watch the finances and do something for sports, I could hold down the lid.

Shortly after that I was elected President of the Commany and have been ever since. The bad eye was gone for keeps but I learned to shoot from the left shoulder and, in time, to putt as well as ever. I still cannot pour a cocktail from a shaker into a glass without missing the glass unless I can bring the glass to touch the lip of the shaker, but fortunately have always been able to have plenty of liquor so a little lost has not been serious, Rachel has become reconciled to stained tables, and I have had the hell of a good time.

When I began to get a bit of pep back one of the first things which bothered me was that I could not shoot. I've always said that when I can't go out into the woods and shoot birds I'm done, and I was not ready for that. I read in some paper how Ben Joy, after having a pellet put out his right eye, learned all over again to shoot from the left shoulder and ended up by winning a national skeet championship. If he could do that I saw no reason why I should not become a passable shot, but it meant practice and lots of it and skeet seemed to be the answer.

Thus skeet came to Hot Springs. It might have come and gone like miniature golf, pitching horseshoes or any other minor sport had it not been for one of the most delightful men it has ever been my privilege to meet. Of course the Scullins had been one of the St. Louis families who came early to Hot Springs and I had long known Charlie Clark, who married Lenore Scullin. Charlie loved to shoot and in his prime was one of the finest shots this country ever produced. He did not like conventions in his shooting any more than in anything else and straight sixteen-yard targets bored him. Skeet had not been developed at this time and the first improvement he made was to mount a hand trap on a rocking chair, which he used to transport to the top of the mountain, and then, with an arrangement of strings, rock the chair and release the trap. That was a lot of fun and, believe me, tricky shooting. Then when skeet was introduced, before it became formalized and was just a way for sportsmen to get a little practice with their field guns, he took that up. Together we located the present field. Charlie designed the trap houses and did the best possible with the shed which was put into service as a club house. In his serious moments he was a competent architect. Grandcharlie, as he was affectionately known by all who shot there, was completely catholic in his shooting friends, and skeet boomed at Hot Springs. We at last got a team of Grandcharlie and four others, which won many shoots throughout the state.

Grandcharlie was a natural, unaffected shot. At the proper time and place he liked a wee nippie and if this came at the end of a shoot he developed a falsetto call for the bird, which we all called his "gin" call. There are a good many of us who would like as much as anything else to hear that call again. He felt he was slipping in later years and made a bet in his sixtieth year that he could shoot five hundred birds in one afternoon, breaking ninety-eight out of the first hundred and not more than one less for each succeeding hundred, the bet being on each individual hundred. He won them all, ending with a ninety-six.

Grandcharlie finally gave up skeet when it became what it is now, a specialized, highly technical game with little relation to the informal play with firearms from which it grew. Once he went to a shoot and was told that by the rules he had to use the ammunition which was sold on the field. That was the last straw. He forfeited his entrance money and never shot in a registered shoot again.

A few years after that Grandcharlie crossed the great divide characteristically. Learning that he had to have an operation, he arranged for the family to go off on a trip, saying nothing about his troubles, then went into the hospital never to come out.

Mrs. Clark gave the Clark Challenge Trophy in his memory, competed for every July. This is a beautiful bowl but I cherished more the tin tea kettles which Grandcharlie used to buy and put up for competition whenever the spirit moved him. Every time I look at one of these I feel it a symbol of true sportsmanship.

## *15. Building the Tower*

M. E. INGALLS was the guiding spirit during the construction of the major portion of the Homestead plant; under M. E. Ingalls, Jr., the east wing, theatre, ballroom, Garden Room and Empire Room were erected; and under my regime the last addition to the hotel building, that of the tower, was carried through. The demand for suites had been steadily growing and many plans for meeting the need for additional rooms were considered, which in the end came down to one of two suggestions, to put additional stories on the existing

building or to put a new structure between the east
wing and the main building, where the ballroom then
stood. The problem was submitted to C. D. Wetmore,
of Warren and Wetmore, an old and constant visitor
at The Homestead and a close personal friend. He
enthusiastically undertook to design the building. One
condition was laid down to which he heartily subscribed,
that whatever was done must be strictly in keeping
with the simple colonial architecture which distinguished
the rest of the hotel.

The tower was built and has been a success since its
opening in the spring of 1929. It is amusing, however, to
find how many people feel they have a proprietary interest in anything which goes on in the Valley. Let a
decaying tree be cut down or the route of a path be
changed and an avalanche of criticism descends on the
management. There was some of this when the tower
was opened but in only one respect was it more than
aversion to something new.

The tower put the final end to a feature which had
been delightful, life on the casino lawn from late afternoon until dusk. The tower was only partially responsible,
for the building of the east wing in 1914 had really sounded
the death knell. Before that the young people, particularly,
used to linger on the lawn until the last rays of the setting
sun left the ridge of the Warm Springs Mountain. The
colors of the slope would fade and the sky, etching the
ridge like a knife, turn to steel gray, with a few wisps of
golden and pink clouds floating above; you could look off
into infinite distance and peace. Having tea with the
girl of the year, with whom you had just been riding,
thoughts of the things you might have said on that ride
would flit through the brain. In after years I have heard
many of those who used to be there say, when faced with

some particularly beautiful prospect, "It gives you the
Ridge feeling, doesn't it?" Now the east wing and tower
pretty well cut off the ridge and their heavy shadows shut
out the soft evening light which used to filter through the
trees on the hill above. The casino lawn is as popular
as ever but not for the twilight hour. There is the same
brilliance in midday but the romance of the gloaming is
gone and those who knew that rightly have an attack of
nostalgia.

When the actual construction of the tower was begun
a troublesome and interesting problem had to be solved
in the matter of foundations. As mentioned before in
discussing the geology of this section, the Valley had once
been the bed of a great river, probably about the close
of the last ice age, which had deposited sediment above
the underlying limestone. However, it had always been
assumed that the ridge on which The Homestead stands
was a spur of limestone extending out from the Warm
Springs Mountain. As a matter of fact such a ledge appears at several points under the main section and it was
assumed this was continuous to the east, but that was not
the case.

When this huge river roared down the Valley there
must have been a pillar of hard limestone jutting up into
a pinnacle at about where the northeast corner of the
main building stands, around which the waters swirled,
carving a mighty canyon to the east toward the mountain
wall. How deep this canyon was we never learned for
when borings were made none of them reached through
the river clay and boulders to solid rock. There is no
particular difficulty in getting satisfactory foundations
for any structure by the use of "floating foundations."
All of the City of Chicago rests on such but while practical,
even if more expensive, there was an added problem in

that the clay on which the mats of steel and concrete, constituting the floating foundation, would rest was not homogeneous.  It was good bearing clay but interspersed with boulders of all sizes, from bowling balls to great masses larger than a cottage.  The small boulders had to be removed and the larger ones incorporated in the foundation mats.  This last demanded skilled engineering for it had to be determined how stable in the clay the boulders themselves were and the effect on their original stability of the added weight of a multistoried steel building.  This delayed construction and increased the cost but it was worked out satisfactorily in the end.

It was obvious that there were going to be many complications in organizing the work so it could go on continuously with the least possible interference with the operations of the hotel.  I think it was Charlie Wetmore who first suggested that if the work was done with the forces of the Virginia Hot Springs Company itself difficulties could be more easily overcome.  W. J. Mathews, chief engineer at the time, felt confident it could be done.  Wetmore had a long talk with Mathews, at the end of which he was convinced the Company forces were competent.  "I like that fellow, Mathews," he said, "he is not afraid of the cars."  I certainly was not, so that is how it was arranged.

Of course the Company's forces had to be greatly expanded, but the nucleus of the construction gang was made up of the same mechanics who constituted the maintenance crew charged with keeping buildings in repair and making the inevitable changes and additions.  No one will ever know if the plan adopted was more economical than if a contractor had been brought in, but it did produce favorable results.  Local mechanics may not be as fast as those of the cities and many are not as skillful, but on the whole they are loyal and try to put out honest work. An amusing result of this way of doing the work is that if any change of a partition or similar job comes up I will find the mechanics milling around before starting work and, when questioned, more often than not one of them will say, "When we built the tower I set the forms for the concrete for this partition; I remember we had trouble with a pipe and shifted it from the way it was shown on the plans." Usually the man is right and, in consequence, a lot of time and money is saved.

# 16. The Open Road

NO ONE ever accepted the doctor's orders—to live out-of-doors, spend as little time in the office as possible and not worry—more completely than I did. With an innate love of the out-of-doors, the thought of the Valley Road sang in my heart to the tune of the Gypsy Baron—"Free as the Wind, the Open Road"—and I took to the forests and streams, to the fields and the air above them as an exile returning home. For a few years we kept our house in the city but in 1925, having sold the place on Long Island, we built

The Yard, the house at Hot Springs in which we now live. I learned a bit about the hotel business, mostly by observation, and plunged wholeheartedly into the other multitudinous activities of the Valley.

One of the first items studied was the water supply. Strangely enough, in what seems to be a well-watered land, the water supply for the Valley is a real problem. The best water, that is the purest and softest, comes from springs on the Warm Springs Mountain at about the 3,000-foot contour, where the overlying sandstone formation meets the basic limestone. A large number of springs had been acquired, the most northerly the one which originally supplied the hotel through wooden pipes, and others to the south, with the most remote about six miles beyond what later became the Cacades golf course. In 1923 the Rubino property was purchased and the huge spring there solved, in quantity, the essential difficulty of adequate volume of water. But this spring had a limestone source and was hard. At about the same time there were rumors that the ridge of the Warm Springs Mountain was going to be sold and I was worried lest the forest cover be cut for grazing, thus possibly diminishing the flow of our high level springs and also creating a source of pollution. In the course of shooting and riding through the woods I had become familiar with the strange formation on top of the mountain, with the two large flats, the "little flat" and the "big flat," the latter of which later was to be the airport. The best geological advice indicated that the source of our springs was the rain which fell on the sandy formation on top of the mountain.

The ridge and for miles to the east was a huge tract of land locally known as the Deeds Country, which had a curious history. Originally it was part of what was known as the Douthat Survey, one of the great land grants of colonial times. It was a wild, inaccessible area with no roads, properly speaking, no schools and just a few scattered clearings. It was covered with forests and was thought to have much valuable lumber; subsequently it developed that due to fires and scattered and irresponsible cutting by squatters there was little left of any value. It was also supposed to have valuable mineral deposits. There is manganese but it occurs in pockets, none sufficiently large to pay for development. Manganese during the first World War, as in the last, was a critical material and the existence of any deposit something to dream about.

Thomas McLaren, who had made a fortune out of Imperial Canadian Cheese, thought there was an investment opportunity and bought the whole survey. What he paid for it I never heard but when he died the property was appraised at upwards of a million dollars. The estate was unwilling to bring Canadian assets to the United States to pay the inheritance tax and, to meet this, borrowed $200,000 from a local syndicate headed by A. C. Ford, of Clifton Forge, giving a mortgage to secure the loan. When this mortgage fell due it became apparent that the value of the property had been greatly exaggerated and the McLaren Estate, after a few years of frantic effort to find a purchaser for the equity, let the property pass to this syndicate. Soon after I came to Hot Springs all sorts of schemes were proposed by this estate and then by the syndicate to get even the mortgage money back. When it became apparent that no complete sale could be made, the syndicate tried to get what they could by selling piecemeal.

In the meantime I had had measurements made of the flow from the various springs along the ridge and on the eastern slope which were at sufficient altitude to make it practical to raise the water over the ridge to Hot Springs. The conclusion was reached that any water rising at 3,000 feet or higher elevation could be used, and I bought for the Company approximately 7,000 acres running along the ridge from Flag Rock, south for about nine miles to include Bald Knob, and down to the 3,000-foot contour on the east and to the cleared land on the Valley side. There was also acquired the right to divert the flow of these springs, particularly those draining into Wilson's Creek to the east, for upwards of ten miles until that joined the Cowpasture River.

It is apparent now that the estimate of a million gallons flow per day, which the engineers reported, was grossly exaggerated. It is also doubtful if it will ever be worth while, in view of later developments in treatment of water, to bring what there is to Hot Springs. However, the purchase of the tract was a good one. The protection of existing water sources was secured, the Valley has been saved from possibly undesirable development on the ridge which overlooks it, a site for an airport was acquired, and some of the loveliest country about here preserved from vandals. Incidentally, there is now going on an interesting lumbering operation by the Company on the eastern side of the ridge. This is being conducted along the best modern forestry principles, under the supervision of the State Conservation Department, leaving the forests in better condition than before cutting. It is apparent that there is a considerable quantity of fine, mature white oak which should be taken out for the health of the forest.

Subsequent to our purchase other moderate-sized tracts were sold out of the survey to individuals. Quite a large portion was sold or given to the state to create the

Douthat State Park, in which an artificial lake has been built. The balance, something like 200,000 acres, has been purchased by Uncle Sam and is now part of the George Washington National Forest.

During the days of the CCC, roads and paths were built through the forest, among others the Skyline Drive along the ridge from where Route 39 crosses the top of Warm Springs Mountain to the McGraw Gap Road, a distance of almost fifteen miles. About two-thirds is on the property of the Company, the balance over government forest and privately owned lands.

During the time of the CCC camps there was one example, amusing if not taken too seriously, of the efficiency of these camps in getting things done. It was during the worst fire season in the last thirty years. One fire, starting east of Route 220 and south of the Cascades, swept up the mountain to Bald Knob. At the same time there were fires on the opposite side of the Valley along Little Mountain. The CCC boys were trying to check the fire along the crest. It was traveling fast and going north toward our property line. Company forces, starting close to Route 220, had run a fire lane along our boundary line up the mountain, coming out on the road to Bald Knob at the first hairpin turn on the final climb to the summit. From the Valley you could see the reflection of the flames in the sky and occasionally the actual blaze as a snag burst into a torch. About 2:00 A. M. I drove up the road toward Bald Knob to check on the situation, stopping at the turn where our fire lane came out. It was pretty smoky and hard to see. The men who had cut the fire lane began drifting in, begrimed and tired. Before coming to this fire they had cut one on Little Mountain, where a fire had been threatening the woods about the Cascades on the west, and had already been on the job continuously for thirty-six hours. I had brought sandwiches and coffee, and a little group formed as, one after another, the patrols drifted up. As we sat around we heard a truck coming down from Bald Knob and soon it appeared through the smoke. A much excited Army captain stopped and said, "All hell's broken loose. I have to take these boys back to camp for they can't stand more. The fire is going over the crest and the whole Deeds Country will burn up. Can't you help?" I asked him how many boys he had and he said two hundred from the Dolly Ann Camp and all who could work from Bath Alum.

Then he rattled off in a great hurry. In the meantime the Company fire crew kept coming in until fifteen were sitting around. I asked Henry Hoover, who was superintendent of such things as forests, if we could give any help. He looked at the tired, grimy men and asked, "How about it, boys?" Twelve of them said they guessed they could go, and I watched them trudge off through the smoke with their fire tools over their shoulders.

That afternoon there was a circus in town and I took the children. I saw one of our fire fighters there, also with his children. "What happened to the fire, Pete?" I asked, wondering why he had quit. "Oh, we cut a good lane, got the backfire going and had it stopped by five o'clock." Twelve men who knew a job had done it, where over three hundred had failed. Of course, there is a good deal of "know how" about fighting fire but it was not all that. The CCC boys would do what they were told but if a spark jumped the backfire they had not enough sense of responsibility to chase over and put it out and the fat would be in the fire all over again.

Having bought the top of the mountain, the next thing to consider was what to do with it. It would make a wonderful place for a golf course, with sandy soil, magnificent views and plenty of water, but the frost does not come out of the ground at that altitude until the middle of May and the mountain is often covered with snow in October so even if cool in summer a course there would not be of much service. A wonderful steeplechase course could be laid out, but that, too, meant a lot of complications.

In the meantime the ever-present search for a landing field went on. There were places in the valleys nearby where sufficient level land was found but always with the difficulty of surrounding mountains necessitating a quick climb. Besides, most of the valleys large enough were near rivers where morning fogs would be a handicap. After the Company acquired the mountain land, fire lanes were cut through it and the chief engineer became familiar with the topography as a result of his studies of water resources. I, too, got to know more about it as a result of grouse shooting. Dave Ingalls flew over it, and it appeared to all of us a possible site for an airport. At first the little flat over the Bear Loop was considered, but the spine of the mountain came up on the western side and there was not enough room. Then we turned to the present location. A platform was built about fifteen feet above the ground so one could see over the area. One day there happened to be at Hot Springs a number of aviation-minded men, Dave Ingalls and some of his friends who had flown with Trubee Davison's Yale Unit during the first World War, including Juan T. Trippe and my friend, Townsend Luddington, who had started the first real Washington-New York air line. We went to the top of the mountain, climbed the platform and, without a dissenting voice, the site for the airport was selected.

Of late years practically all construction by the Company has been by its own forces and generally well done. The building of the airport, however, was a pretty amateurish job. The use of bulldozers and similar equipment was not as widespread in 1930 as it has since become nor did the Company at that time own sufficient of such machines. The airport, for another reason, was largely built by hand labor. The depression had started but no one thought it was going to continue. It was then, however, more acute in Bath and Highland Counties than at later periods. The Warm Springs Bank had failed, resulting in direct loss to many and for others demands that loans, which had been regarded as more or less permanent, be paid. But the worst of the suffering came as a result of drought. The farming economy hereabout is based on livestock, with farmers taking advantage of natural bluegrass pastures and only growing enough grain to winter their animals. Pastures dried up and the grain crop was a failure. Farmers who had bought feeding stock found themselves under the necessity of buying feed. Many who had never been in debt before borrowed to make the purchases and then, when the price of cattle dropped, found that on forced sale even the cost of feed could not be recovered, let alone that of the cattle. As a result there was much suffering and unemployment.

The financial affairs of the Company were none too rosy and the work at the airport might well have been stopped, but people did not realize the long, hard years ahead and employment could be offered on top of the mountain, so the work went on. Barracks were built and construction proceeded all winter. Anyone who worked through those months earned his pay. The road along the ridge was little more than a path and there can still be seen openings crisscrossing along the ridge where trucks forced their way through the underbrush when the road proper became impassable by reason of snow or mud. The first job, of cutting the brush, was all done by hand. One December day I went up to look things over. The thermometer was just above zero. Driving around in a Model A Ford, one of the tires was punctured by a "stob" left from cutting brush. In the bitter cold the jack snapped when I tried to change the tire. I got help from the gang at work and saw one of the most remarkable feats of strength I have ever witnessed. No other jack was available so Arch Adams, one of the men, said he would hold up the car wheel while the tire was changed. Only one man could get a grip and in that bitter cold he held the wheel off the ground while the damaged tire was removed and the spare applied.

The original plans for the airport have never really been completed. These called for transverse runways as well as the T which now exists, elaborate hangars and extensions of runways to take the largest commercial planes.

Aviation has always had a persuasive advocate at Hot Springs in the person of David Ingalls, who began flying in World War I, when he became a Naval ace, and has continued ever since. He practically never comes to Hot Springs except by plane. During the Hoover administration he was Assistant Secretary of the Navy for Aviation and while stationed in Washington frequently left his office after opening his mail, stopped over at Hot Springs for luncheon and a couple of sets of tennis or a round of golf, then continued on to his home in Cleveland for a late afternoon polo game. One of the things he early tried to do for aviation was to establish emergency fields on routes from Hot Springs east and west. Some farmers were not cooperative and that fact came to the attention of Ed Porter, who had on his farm on the Cowpasture River large, level fields. Ed wrote me a letter which I passed on to Dave, and the public relations officer of the Navy seized on it. Nothing relating to Hot Springs, not even the accounts of the Japanese internees or the first World Food Conference, ever had such publicity as this letter, which was printed in every paper in the country; it reads as follows:

"DEAR MR. INGALLS:

I notice a good many planes going over. Now you tell those people if they have any trouble of any kind and it might be unsafe to go on with only woodland from my place to landing, to land anywhere on me regardless of crops—you know, with any rain at all, we can grow a crop in three months, but it takes twenty-one years to grow a man. Still some are not worth a damn after grown. I have plenty of level land to make a safe landing in case of accident.

Yours truly,

E. S. PORTER."

## *17. Farming and Forestry*

THE SOIL and all it means has always had a fascination for me and, when I came to Hot Springs to live, the discovery that I was to be responsible for farming operations on a considerable scale was exciting and pleasing. Hot Springs is far removed from any market center and since the earliest times the hotels in the Valley have relied on local sources for much of the food products they required. A hundred and twenty-five years ago venison and wild turkeys were standard articles of food. A traveler in 1833, speaking of

Warm Springs, said, "The table is well furnished with all varieties of flesh and fowl in common use, to which may be added a constant supply of fresh venison from the adjacent mountains." The days when game could supply the larder soon passed but until the railway came to the Valley practically all perishable foods had to be produced right at home. Much of this food was and still is purchased from farmers along the Valley Road but when the new owners acquired the properties in 1889 they found they were willy-nilly in the farming business as well as tavern keepers.

The one product impossible to purchase locally, and at the same time almost the foundation of catering, was milk and, in consequence, the Company had its own dairy. The whole agricultural operation is built about this, directly or indirectly. The original location was on the Warm Springs Mountain at the end of the road which crosses the seventeenth fairway from the Valley Road. Early in the present century the shortage of pasture there led to moving the barns and other buildings to what is now the ball park. The barns at the old dairy were preserved and have been rebuilt several times, now serving to house a flock of purebred sheep.

When the move was made to the ball park location an attempt was made to modernize the plant and improve the herd. At that time the policy of buying purebred bulls was inaugurated but most unfortunately cows were selected at random, simply buying good individuals and trying to keep the herd balanced about equally between Guernsey and Holstein types. As a result of continuous use of purebred bulls, by 1943, when the holocaust of Bangs disease struck, necessitating the destruction of more than half the herd, the heifers of that year had less than one-fourth of one per cent of common blood. In type the Guernseys and Holsteins were as true as in any purebred herd but they could not be registered and the bull calves had to be sold as veal, only for want of papers. In rebuilding the herd after the elimination of Bangs, the cattle shortage made it necessary to buy any good, sound milking cows, and the herd has not as yet recovered its class.

The ball park location did not prove a favorable one for the dairy. The limestone of the Valley stops at Little Mountain and the skeet field, which was the pasture, lies on sandstone and shale. The land is not fertile and in dry weather the pasturage dries up. In 1928 the dairy was again moved, to its present location near Warm Springs. This time a really modern plant was built. While modern in every way when erected, it has had to be changed continuously to keep up with progress. One interesting example is the matter of mechanical milking. This was installed in the new buildings but taken out after a few years' trial as it did not seem possible to maintain satisfactory sanitation with the machines. The art improved and in 1946 a new and improved type of mechanical milker was installed and has so far proved highly satisfactory.

There are about one hundred and ten milking animals in our herd and about half that many heifers or cows turned out between milking periods. So far as possible, feed is produced on the arable land of the Company. The requirements of crop rotation as well as the growing of feed for dairy cattle makes a considerable amount of roughage available as a by-product. To utilize this, sheep farming has come in. We have had a rather discouraging experience with sheep so far as the use of purebred animals is concerned. Financially, in comparison with other farming operations, sheep are the most profitable. We started out with one flock of purebred animals and another, of substantially the same size, of good, sound grades. We run about three hundred and fifty breeding ewes, and if there is any difference in the quality or quantity of the lambs or wool produced by the two flocks no accounting has been able to show it; and the half-breds seem to be a bit hardier.

Another use for roughage is in buying and feeding steers. Near the great cattle country of Highland County, we are able to buy these advantageously. Starting in a small way and only fattening them on grass during the summer, now the farm has learned to produce high class beef. It is hard to say if this beef business is profitable or not. One of the hardships of rationing which seemed rather unfair was that had the Company, during the beef shortage, been allowed to slaughter and use the beef raised on its own farm as a by-product The Homestead would never have been short of red meat. As the regulations were drawn, however, the hotel could not use its own meat and, what was worse, the cost of marketing was so great that it did not pay to fatten. So when meat was shortest the Company farms produced less beef than at any time in the last thirty years.

We also have quite a number of hogs, which are fed on the skim milk from the dairy and on swill from the hotel. These hogs are good only for the cash they bring on the markets, for it does not pay to feed the grain necessary to produce the high-class pork needed by the hotel.

I thought when I came to Hot Springs that I knew something about farming. Now, after twenty-five years of experience, I am beginning to learn how to begin to learn what I thought I knew. Sad to relate, the education has been costly. We tried chicken farming for many years, almost fifteen in fact. The experiment resulted in the loss of an average of $7,000 a year but it did provide fresh eggs for The Homestead which could not be obtained elsewhere at that time. A few years before the war sources of fresh eggs were found and the chicken farm abandoned. That was just the wrong time for if it had been continued during the war and subsequently the black figures would have been large enough to wipe out the previous losses.

Our most colossal failure, however, was the attempt to have a vegetable farm on the Barney Johnson farm, which had to be purchased in connection with the use of the water from the Cascades stream at Hot Springs. Tenant houses were built and a water line from a spring in Healing Springs Gap, two miles away, was laid for irrigation. In neither quality nor quantity was there ever satisfactory production. Now this farm raises alfalfa, corn and grain for the dairy and beef herd.

When the dairy was moved to its present location it afforded an opportunity for a wonderful party, mostly engineered by my brother, George. The second story of the large barn has an immense, unobstructed floor. I took George over to see it and he at once said, "What a fine place for a real barn dance!" He wanted to make this a full day so a picnic supper was held on Flag Rock, then the multitude adjourned to the dairy for a dance. No produce had been put into the barn as yet except a few oats, the handling of which had given just enough polish to the floor to make it good for dancing. It certainly was a festive occasion. It was a warm evening, the dancing was active and the large double doors on the second floor, through which the barn could be filled, were opened by someone for ventilation and why no one danced right out to a twenty-foot drop I don't know.

I remember that Bill Flynn, the architect for the Cascades golf course, was present and every one of the two hundred and fifty pounds of him had a wonderful time. He was probably saved by the mint juleps on Flag Rock early in the evening, for when he arrived at the barn he was hardly skipping about. In the middle of the evening, being more or less responsible for the property, I became panic-stricken over the fire hazard. That cramped my personal style and formed the basis for the taboo on further affairs at that location, but it was a great party.

Closely akin to farming is forestry. Of the seventeen thousand and more acres owned by the Company probably ten thousand are in forest cover. These forests are a valuable asset both for the lumber they provide and for such incidental benefits as protection of watershed and recreation, this last, after all, the main business of the Company.

Few people appreciate how the character of forests has changed during the past fifty years. Of course there is the obvious alteration resulting from ruthless lumbering, uncontrolled fires and, to a minor extent, clearing for agriculture. About here the latter is a minor factor for during this time probably more farm land has been abandoned in Bath and Highland Counties than has been brought under cultivation. The earliest change was the destruction of much of the pine timber. When I first came to know these mountains one of the striking features was the large number of huge dead pines still standing. In many cases it was difficult to tell definitely what variety these were; I have an idea they were mostly pitch, but many may have been white pines. These remnants, many five and more feet in diameter, showed that there must have been a much heavier stand of pine around the middle of the last century than at present;

instead of a comparatively small proportion of the trees being conifers they must have constituted a large part of the forest cover. These old snags showed the working of bark beetles and old-timers said that an epidemic of beetles was what decimated the conifers, particularly the pines. The pines are now coming back, which seems to prove that the explanation given for this infestation was the correct one.

The chief protection a pine has against the Ips and similar beetles is by drowning the insect with its sap. Before the development of the Forest Service fires were rampant throughout the Appalachians. These fires undoubtedly weakened the trees when they did not kill them, and with lowered vitality they had less sap. Worse than that, these fires destroyed the ground litter, permitting the surface soil to dry, thus cutting off the water from which sap was formed. Such conditions upset the balance between the beetles and the trees. Once this balance was gone the trees had little chance. Dead or dying trees afforded a home and food for beetles and the number increased in geometrical proportion until soon even thriving trees were overwhelmed. In the last twenty-five years fires have been less widespread and destructive. Either that or a natural cycle has cut down the beetle population, for while occasional beetle damage is seen it is now usually limited. For example, though some of the climax trees in the lovely stand of white pine along the Katydid Trail show beetle infestation, most are free and thriving.

The greatest change in the forests came with the chestnut blight. Over huge areas chestnut was the dominant species. In the nineties anyone standing in front of The Homestead on a midsummer day and looking toward the Warm Springs Mountain might have thought there had been a snowfall, so completely did the white chestnut bloom cover the slopes. The chestnuts are now all gone; occasionally a sprout, particularly at the higher altitudes, will grow large enough to bear a few burrs but these die when from two to three inches in diameter. The death of the chestnuts also wrought havoc with other trees not affected by the blight. Sunlight was let in where there had been deep shade, thus changing the environment. Then, too, the dead trees harbored all sorts of borers which, like the Ips beetle, increased beyond the capacity of the trees, birds and other enemies to keep them in check, and healthy trees were attacked.

All of these misfortunes have changed the forests. There are still a few places where a climax forest can be seen. The best of these is in the Cascades Gorge where the stand is of mixed growth; on the ridge south of the Cascades stream below the first bridge it is of white oak, and also on the eastern slope of the Warm Springs Mountain and along the headwaters of Wilson's Creek.

I was hardly used to the idea of being a part of the Hot Springs Company before I became immensely interested in forestry and had a young man, trained at the Cornell School of Forestry, survey our woods. In a way, his report was discouraging. To take out the mature timber was uneconomical with the then price of lumber, and so far as replanting areas where the pine and chestnut were gone, except in the case of abandoned fields it was both unnecessary, as natural reforestation would do the job, and exceedingly expensive. Some things were done, however. Over a million trees were planted and, generally speaking, with great success. Mistakes were made, such as planting many Scotch pines around the golf links; while these have done well they are peculiarly subject to beetles and have not thrived as have the red and white pine. A great disappointment was the attempt to replant the "Little Flat" near the airport; a most destructive fire had gone over this, wiping out all vegetation and leaving black, ash-strewn ground in its wake. (Incidentally, this was the only time I was ever in difficulty at a forest fire, almost being caught between two blazes.) This seemed to offer an unequalled opportunity to replant, and about a hundred thousand pines were set out. The loss here was greater than with all the other plantings; blackjack oak, laurel and rhododendron came in so fast and thickly that the little seedlings never got a start and now only an occasional small, stunted pine can be found.

Another venture was the removal of dead chestnut. It is not valuable lumber and while we cut and sawed much (the framing of our house, The Yard, is almost all chestnut) there was really no market. Most of the dead trees went to extract plants and hundreds of carloads were shipped out. Except for long-range planning this was not a profitable operation, which probably accounts for the fact that not many other landowners salvaged their dead chestnut. When someone would contract to take out the trees, and, where the rub came, clean up afterwards to prevent fire hazard, I closed the deal even if payments for the wood were not enough to cover the wages of the men we employed to see that the work was done properly. We still have some standing dead chestnut and every now and then take some out. One rather picturesque feature of the landscape is passing with the chestnut for those were the trees which furnished the rails for snake fences.

We have made some effort to bring back chestnuts and one of the first plantings of the Chinese blight-resistant variety was made along the South Walking

Trail, with stock furnished by the United States Forestry Service. These trees have been growing long enough to produce substantial crops but the nuts are wormy and the trees are now old enough so that it can be seen that they are more like bushes and will never develop into real forest trees like the natives. About five years ago a small number of a different variety, which the authorities thought would make better trees, was obtained. I made the terrible mistake of telling where the first transplants were put and the following year someone else had them all. Later we obtained others, which were planted under conditions which should induce a more tree-like growth, but this time the location is being kept a dark secret.

We have learned a good deal in our forestry experiments. Some things are a bit surprising. I still believe forest cover is necessary to protect the flow of springs but I know of one spring, flowing strongly enough to justify half a mile of pipe to bring it into our water supply, which has completely dried up since the fields above it have gone back to forest. I also know that, in spite of the talk of conservationists, even with the present high prices of lumber, the costs of selective cutting and clearing up after such an operation are so great that there is small profit in it. In the long run what is called scientific lumbering may pay off. It will for the country as a whole, but for the small holder the only way to make a profit is by ruthless, indiscriminate, clean cutting. This is regrettable but means there should be a certain amount of sympathy for the farmer who has only a few hundred acres of timber.

Although I never knew the actual figures, I think the effort to cut with due regard to the forest cost the Tide Water Oil Company huge sums before they were

through with their extensive operations at Bacova, now
a ghost town only kept alive by the housing shortage in
the Valley.

## *18. The Valley Made*
## *The Homestead*

**T**HE CAPTION to this chapter is almost literally true. Earlier in this book I have told how the immensely complicated building of the tower was done by the forces of the Company. These forces have been recruited in overwhelming proportion from those born and bred along the Valley Road or its extensions. Many coming to The Homestead for a first visit remark on how well it fits into its environment—it not only fits in but is actually a part of it. No top management could possibly have brought about such conformity by orders; it came because the work done was by the hands and the brains of those who belonged to the land.

It is generally true that the characteristics of a population are largely determined by its physiographical surroundings. A mountain land, where effort is required for satisfactory living, breeds fine men and women and, if that land also has natural beauty, something besides the sterner virtues as well. I may be prejudiced because I have lived so many years on the Valley Road and have come to love its hills and dales and the people who live among them, but, having seen a good deal of the rest of the world, my judgment is not to be entirely despised and I rate the raw material of these mountain people near the top.

The policy of using local labor as well as nature's resources has paid big dividends. Not only has home talent furnished material which has been developed into skilled artisans but this practice has assured continuity and a knowledge of our properties which is invaluable.

Earlier, in speaking of the building of the tower, I mentioned how a workman recalled that actual construction varied from the plans. A few days before this was written there was a similar incident. When the state took over the toll road to Warm Springs we deeded to them a lot of valuable rights of way including that through Hot Springs. As an additional consideration the state paid the cost of the wall around cottage row, built by our masons. When the new roadway was laid by the kitchen entrance someone had the bright idea of running a conduit under it in case the telephone lines to Healing Springs were ever put underground. The conduit was put in but no reliable record of its location kept, and this year when we were ready to put in the underground cable we had nothing to show where it ran. However, one of the employees of the powerhouse had been a labor boss when the road was laid and remembered to a foot where the conduit came through.

Excepting during the most crowded times, the Company employs about as many people, as mechanics or in connection with maintenance of farm and garden, water supply, telephones and a host of other activities, as it does for the actual operation of the hotel. Many of these have worked for the Company all their lives and, in addition, the number of members of the same families always on the pay roll is surprising. The classic example of this is the Keyser family. When my father was in charge he sent for the pay roll one day and after looking at it, accused the chief engineer of padding the rolls. "There couldn't be thirty-seven Keysers working for us," he said. But the records were right. I don't know how many there are today, but a lot, so many in fact that you are not taking a long chance if you greet a passer-by as Keyser. While there are probably more of the Keyser family than any other, they are only one such instance. Locally it is said "The Keysers came before the Indians." There are many other names which for more than fifty years have appeared continuously on our pay rolls.

If natural that such labor should be drawn from local sources, it is perhaps a bit surprising that the hotel itself is so largely staffed in the same manner. It is difficult to think of anything more foreign to the tradition and environment of the dwellers along the Valley Road than what is required in operating a hotel. Nevertheless, with the exception of the colored help, an overwhelming proportion of those staffing the hotel come from this source, and this is true throughout the organization. It might be thought simple for farmers' wives and daughters to learn to work as maids, but even the technical positions, requiring training and executive ability, are filled by men and women who come from families either denizened in the Valley for generations or from neighboring localities with the same background. For example, the comptroller of the Company, assistant secretary, assistant managers, the steward, general cashier, housekeeper, purchasing agent, farm manager, head of the livery, and many others of the higher hierarchy of the organization are Virginia mountaineers, most of them born within a few miles of Hot Springs. This has come about because as far back as 1891 the policy was formulated of giving preference to residents when taking on new employees. The custom went farther, for it was early recognized that, due to its location, The Homestead must be self-sufficient, and every effort was made to find a job for any promising boy or girl, in the hope of discovering talent.

Few of the Company's many colored employees are indigenous for not many negroes live in Western Virginia. However, The Homestead has been fortunate in the colored force which has been brought in. Many now own their own homes near Hot Springs and others, to the fourth generation in at least one instance have, since they first came, lived in quarters furnished by the Company. Among these are many employees who are away for longer or shorter periods during the dull seasons, but each year's pay roll, including these, shows a remarkable repetition of names.

It is not only a stupid but an evil employer who seeks to capitalize on loyalty from those who work for him. It should never be counted upon but if it does come there can be nothing more gratifying to the man who receives it. It was the loyalty of its personnel which saved the Company in the trying times of the thirties when, if ever, there was a temptation to desert what looked like a sinking ship. I personally might have been better off materially if I had shaken off responsibilities and quit; when one after another, in all ranks, stood steadfast and expressed their trust in me, such a course was simply unthinkable.

After I came to Hot Springs I became involved in two matters, not directly connected with The Homestead or the Company but from which I gained much insight into the community life of the Valley. Their story will help in an understanding of the background against which The Homestead is set; these were the Bath County National Bank and the *Bath County Enterprise*, a weekly newspaper.

From earliest times there had been an effort to establish a bank in Hot Springs. This was of importance to the Company, with a pay roll of around one hundred thousand dollars a month and monthly trade bills of a similar amount, which could not be handled efficiently without a local checking account. For a time after my arrival it was attempted to carry on operations by using banks in Covington for most purposes but that was awkward. Furthermore the complications provided an opportunity for one cashier to take upward of $20,000 of our money which he promptly invested in German marks, leaving no salvage.

The Warm Springs Bank failed and this failure was more or less cataclysmic for the economy of the county. Inextricably tied up with the failure was a shortage in the County Treasurer's office of almost a hundred thousand dollars. Country folk are prone to speak of the corruption of large cities, but this defalcation amounted to practically one year's tax levy, which, proportionately, makes the takings of the Tweed Ring in New York look like small potatoes.

I say, advisedly, that the shortage and the bank failure were inextricably mixed up, for I had to devote a lot of hard work to finding out just what happened. When the State Auditor discovered the shortage a special grand jury was empaneled and I was named foreman. As a practicing lawyer I had, of course, never been on a jury but was not disqualified in Virginia as I had never been admitted to the bar here although in good standing in New York and with the Supreme Court of the United States. I did not argue my qualifications, both from curiosity to see how a jury worked and from a desire to have the truth brought out. I never found out what happened. From all I could gather, Houston Byrd, prosecuting attorney and the leading politician of the county, and Venable, the County Treasurer, lost a lot of money in a scheme for an oil distributing company and got the cash by juggling the accounts of the bank and the county. Byrd was dead, the County Treasurer refused to testify, and the one witness who I felt sure knew the whole story blankly "Could not remember." I tried to get the witness committed for contempt but you cannot prove someone does remember when they say they don't, so only the fact of the shortage could be proved, not how it came about. We did indict the Treasurer and he was tried and sentenced to a year in jail. I believe this was one of the very few convictions of a county treasurer as a result of T. Coleman Andrews' audit of the accounts of all county treasurers in the State, although some twenty-five per cent were found irregular. On the whole, I did not feel my work was wasted although all was not accomplished we hoped for.

More than the loss to the county, which was not fully covered by bond, I regretted that the affair was indirectly the cause of the death of one of the finest gentlemen it has ever been my privilege to meet. J. Ed Gillett was a mountaineer with all the good qualities of his ilk and none of the bad. He was a magnificent woodsman, his character such that he had an outstanding position in the county, particularly among those untouched by the progress of such centers as Hot Springs, and had been made a director of the Bank of Warm Springs. Ed had just sold the last of his timber and put the proceeds into a new house. This dwelling did not have the charm of the old one but was modern and the pride of his eye. The crash took everything Ed had and that, plus the feeling of responsibility for what had happened, broke his heart and he died shortly after. The Gilletts lived about twenty miles from Hot Springs and one of the finest riding jaunts was to their home, where Mrs. Gillett provided wonderful meals, with marvelous preserves. Both as Ed's wife and for herself, Mrs. Gillett had a host of friends, and I was pleased to find a way for her to get along by putting her in charge of the women's locker room at the Casino, where she still presides.

The Bath County National at Hot Springs was the last of the banks in the Valley. It had been run pretty much on a friendly basis and while there was nothing wrong the bank did not inspire confidence. Fortunately just at that time Captain William Talbott retired from active affairs and came to Hot Springs to live. He was soon elected to the board and rapidly put its affairs in order. Captain Talbott was an army man who had made a fortune after the Spanish War, installing the telephone system in Cuba, and when he came to Hot

Springs still had plenty of energy. One of the ironies of fate is that although building up the local bank he, at the same time, personally invested heavily in the Harriman National Bank of New York and on its collapse was almost ruined.

C. S. Andersen and I were also elected to the board and, while our services were mostly to support Talbott, it was not long before the affairs of the bank were in satisfactory condition.

I knew almost nothing about technical banking but took this work seriously and that entailed gaining considerable knowledge of how the Valley people lived and who were the leading citizens. The bank did some mercantile banking but mostly loans were personal or to farmers. Obviously, we had to find out just how a man could make a living on a mountain farm.

I suppose every bank gets some bad loans but on the whole I found that character loans, if you knew the people, were surprisingly safe in this community. It was interesting to discover the universality of banking problems. The bank had one slow but well secured loan amounting to considerable money. One evening the head of one of the largest banks in the country dined with me and wanted to talk about the mountain people. I told him about this loan, and he remarked that the world was the same all over. He had the same problem in New York except that there some six more zeros had to be added to the sums involved.

The Bath County National Bank today, with deposits of two million dollars, is as sound as any country bank can be, with its chief difficulty that of finding borrowers who will bring in sufficient income to pay expenses. The work on the bank emphasized how much Bath County depends on the Virginia Hot Springs Company. Even including the area east of the Warm Springs Valley, with a somewhat different economy, there are only approximately eight thousand inhabitants in the county, about the same number there were one hundred years ago. The Company employs, on the average, just under a thousand people. In all the county there is not a single business, except the Company, with more than fifteen employees. Taking into account the proportion of Company employees, dependent members of their families and those performing services for these, it is obvious that almost half the population depends directly on the Company. In addition, with the policy of buying farm produce locally whenever possible, there is not much to county economics except the Company. It is gratifying that this situation is appreciated by the county people, whom I have found almost universally sympathetic with Company problems. It can be noted again that the Company and its environment are one and the same.

Captain Talbott was a delightful gentleman but when he came to Hot Springs still had traces of an army ramrod up his backbone and at times was a bit shocked at some of my casualness. When Baron Rosenkrantz died we were both asked to be pallbearers. The services were held at Roseloe and then the cortege moved on to the Warm Springs cemetery. McKee Dunn was another of the pallbearers, and he and Talbott got in my car to go to the cemetery. McKee and I had made some concession to the occasion by wearing dark suits but Talbott had on his cutaway. He got into the back seat and McKee and I in front. The cortege moved slowly and to avoid boredom McKee turned on the car radio. It was October, 1933, and a world series ball game was being played between the Giants and Senators. That game was a classic and the broadcast exciting. I could not get out of the line of cars

to listen and the game got more and more tense. As we
turned from the highway into the cemetery drive Hubbell
was on the mound, with three balls and two strikes on the
batter, a man on base and the score tied. At that moment
Talbott reached over and turned the radio off, with the
remark that he did not think it quite respectful to drive
up to the grave with it going. I fear I used some pretty
strong language, and for quite a while felt a chill in the
air whenever I met Talbott.

Talbott died suddenly and some loose ends still had
to be picked up by Harry Cavendish, who succeeded him
and is still president of the bank, with myself a sort of
nominal vice president.

*The Bath County Enterprise* brought me even closer
to the life of the Valley. This was a weekly newspaper
published in the Valley since 1897. It was owned locally
and had had a varied career, when the owners fell for a
high-pressure circulation promoter and came a final
cropper. The office was in a sort of lean-to, with a lot
of junk machinery. One day I heard that the paper had
come to the end of its string, that the Linotype was to be
taken away for failure to meet payments to the manu-
facturer, and that the rest of the equipment was to be
sold for junk. My brother, Albert, happened to come into
the office and I told him what was going to happen, saying
I thought it was a calamity as there was no other paper
in the county, it had been published for such a long time,
and filled a real need in the community. Albert asked why
I did not buy it and I replied that I didn't have the money
—it would take about $15,000 to pay debts, put it on its
feet, etc.—and besides I had so many different kinds of
jobs I was not looking for the sort of headache produced
by the newspaper business. Albert said nothing more but

that evening, as we were playing bridge, remarked casually, "Fay, I bought the *Enterprise* this afternoon."

Naturally I was astonished, but my first reaction was to say, "You haven't got me in for anything, have you?"

Then he proudly explained that he had bought it without putting up a cent. He settled with the creditors by promising them stock in a new corporation he was going to form, and agreed to endorse the note for the Linotype. "You are to have nothing to do with it except that you are to write a column for it weekly." Probably, as when I took over the real management of the hotel later on, I would have refused had I known as much as I do now, though I am not sure for I have enjoyed the contact the column has brought with the Valley people. Anyway, beginning the next week, I undertook it. In the first year or so Albert wrote for perhaps three or four issues but, with that exception, save when the paper had to suspend for a time during the war, my column has been in every week when the rest of the paper was set to go. That did not always mean Wednesday, for the publication date was Thursday; the *Enterprise* often had the unique distinction of publishing tomorrow's news yesterday. It was always dated Thursday but until quite recently it was a red-letter day if it got out before Saturday.

The full story of the *Enterprise* would justify a book in itself. Troubles came soon. Albert hired a girl to help, and the owner of the shack where the paper was published discovered the girl had slipped from virtue and announced the lease would be canceled if she was not immediately discharged. In the vernacular, that "burned Albert up." He had to skip an issue, but then rented the premises of the defunct Warm Springs Bank and went ahead. Later he bought that building for the paper.

My youngest daughter, Susie, had the journalistic bug and when, on graduating at the top of her class at Bryn Mawr, she could not, because of the war, take advantage of the year's study in Europe awarded in consequence, she succeeded in persuading the college authorities to allow her to substitute a year's scholarship at the University of Missouri's School of Journalism. Susie then came back and took over the *Enterprise*, of which Albert ultimately made her a present, and had it pretty well on the road to prosperity when marriage and babies put an end to her journalistic career—she owns it, but as an absentee landlord.

My column still goes on, and its reception by the mountain people has added to an understanding of them. At the start I said I would not do the job if it meant consideration for the toes I might tread on. I was to be free to write on any subject and in any vein I might choose. This I have done, and the acceptance of this policy has been remarkable.

I had only been writing the column for a year or so when the Ku Klux Klan started activities near Hot Springs. I minced no words, although I knew some influential people were members. One day Albert and I took a drive into the backwoods. We got into a cul-de-sac, with the only way out a barred gate by a farmhouse. I thought we were in a pickle, for this farmer was a member of the Klan and undoubtedly had been offended by what I had written. Albert had a way of doing things and explaining afterward and before I could even think he was out of the car and walking up to the house. The farmer came out and Albert, introducing himself, asked about opening the gate. "Be you the fellow that writes them articles in the *Enterprise?*" was the reply.

Albert admitted he owned the paper but said the author of the articles was in the car. With that the old man said, "I want to shake him by the hand. I don't agree with all he writes, some of the things he writes about are none of his business, but, by God, he don't mince matters and you know he tells what he thinks is the truth."

We had met a Voltaire in the wilderness.

While this was the most dramatic instance, the times I have stopped, while shooting or just rambling about the country, at a house far off the beaten track and been told how much my column was valued are too numerous to mention. Such things as this have meant even more to me than Frank Kent's wife writing that she thought my handling of some subject was better than her husband's. I have never written up or down to my readers and have covered every subject my imagination suggested, from the change of location of a local road to the raising of sugar cane in Java, or the political organization of the Assyrians. I have enjoyed it but have learned that besides death and taxes there is a third inexorable, and that is the date line for a columnist. For almost twenty years I have tried to get one or two pieces in reserve but without the thought that the thing is going to be read immediately it is impossible to write with conviction.

## *19. The Little White Pill Comes to the Valley*

IHAVE met few men in my life who I could say were truly geniuses. One of these was a German, born in Hanover. His earliest recollection was of his family fleeing when the Prussians came in 1870 and to his death he carried an undying hatred of the Prussians. He was brought to America and became a mechanical engineer where, with the more than human machines he devised, he made possible one of the great metal-working industries of his adopted country. When the first war came along he was torn between loyalty to his adopted country and hatred of the Prussians on one hand and love of the fatherland on the other. The first motives triumphed and he performed miracles for the Allies, but divided loyalties and frenzied labors were too much for him and he broke down. I got to know him pretty well and found he was getting into the hands of quack doctors.

At that time I knew Dr. James, one of the leading physicians in New York, and also was aware that, like so many physicians, he was fascinated with metal working machines and in fact had a sort of laboratory-machine shop at his place on Long Island, where he amused himself making instruments for his profession. I told him about Mueller and roused his interest and, after much trouble, finally got Mueller to consult him. After that I lost touch with Mueller for almost a year and then one day he walked into my office, looking like a new man, and told me his story: "I went to see your friend but thought he was just like the rest of them. I was sure of it when he got up after making his examination and said he was going into the next room to get a pill which would cure me. He said I must take it at least three times a week and, if I would, I would not worry about anything else and would get well. I was disgusted. He came back and handed me two pills about an inch in diameter, and what do you think they were—GOLF BALLS! I was mad but gave them a chance and, do you know, they really cured me."

A spa ought to have all possible facilities for helping people to regain health and, as Mueller found out, golf is one of these. Driving through the Valley now one will see plenty of these little pills being knocked about by otherwise sensible men and women on the courses at Hot

Springs and the Cascades and also in the bluegrass pastures by small boys, white and colored, who have been given a club by their players, which they swing with an abandon their elders can never attain. The whole Valley has become golf-minded.

Not only was golf a necessity for a spa but the bug with which I was infected on the Montague meadows was transmitted to my father.

As has been so often reiterated in Homestead advertising, a course was laid out with the first tee placed just where it is today. It was a funny little six-hole course in the beginning, but bear in mind that was the day of the gutta ball and distances were different when measured in terms of how far a ball could be driven. The first green was under the walnut tree on the present first fairway, with a stone wall just beyond it which had to be surmounted for the second hole. There was a long discussion over the cost of removing these stones to improve play, which seems amusing when one thinks of the hundred yards of six-foot culvert installed recently in the sixth fairway at the Cascades with hardly a thought, much of it requiring rock excavation.

Naturally no one knew much about golf when those first six holes were laid out and people began knocking balls about, but in 1899 the Virginia Hot Springs Golf and Tennis Club was formed. There were mighty few golf clubs in the country and precedent was lacking for its various functions. One of the first seemed to be the adoption of insignia and colors. In those days and for many years thereafter no Englishman thought it respectable to play golf without wearing a coat. Our climate hardly permitted tweeds while exercising in the hot sun and as a compromise a blazer was designed. Perhaps because the most formalized sporting attire was the pink coat of the fox-hunter, those early coats were of red, with the collar and cuffs in club colors. Clubs still adopt colors and members wear sort of blazers trimmed with these but it is many years since I have seen anyone wearing one while playing. For a long time those who organized the club went around in hot, brilliant red coats, to the envy of the younger generation, not thought of sufficient age and importance to merit such finery.

It was next decided that the club must have a professional. Every golf course had to have one but there were not many to choose from. While living at White Sulphur we had run across a most delightful Englishman, Herbert A. C. Beauclerk, reputedly a younger son of the Duke of St. Albans. He was a charming gentleman, about all that a cultured Englishman should be and, perhaps in consequence, capable in many ways except in earning a living. At this time Beauclerk was living with the Rumbolds and pretty well down and out. He was eking out a bare existence as a shepherd, just about able to keep body and soul together. Dr. Brandt, Fred Sterry and my father became fond of him and considered long to find some sort of a job which would let him get along. One of the caddies was being used as a professional but more than that was needed and Beauclerk was suggested for the position. He knew nothing about golf but the combination of an Englishman of the old school tie tradition and a love of all sports seemed to spell golf, and Beauclerk was approached with the proposal that he be put in charge. It was probably the best job he had ever been offered and he accepted. Beauclerk never did learn much about the game but made a brave effort. Somehow he got hold of a book on golf and diligently conned it. When he gave lessons he would carry the book and refer to it while the pupil swung the club. I do not know what this book was but it is of interest to note that even that far back books were being written about the Royal and Ancient Game.

Beauclerk was a man about five feet eleven, weighing not more than one hundred and forty pounds. His legs and arms were put on as they are in spidery drawings of children, all angles, no curves and attached at odd points—no curves is not altogether true for there was a bow in the legs from long association with a saddle. He was an accomplished horseman, an excellent shot and by long odds the finest fly fisherman that in years of association with that genus I have ever run across. Weir Mitchell, who was more than a great physician, became a close friend of Beauclerk and ultimately built for him the cottage called Beauclerk Lodge, at the location of the Shriver cottage. Beauclerk lived here for many years, a joy to his friends and a treat to all who came to Hot Springs.

Naturally, attractive as Beauclerk was and as satisfactory in charge of golf, there had to be someone who really knew a bit about the game. He struggled manfully but if a motion picture could have been preserved of his contortions it would well have illustrated the couplet:

"S is the swing you learn in the books
But, Oh, if you could only see how it looks."

"Wulla" Park had about this time won the British Open Championship, one of the first to do so, and came to this country to cash in on the achievement, just as is done today. He was brought to Hot Springs as the pro, leaving Beauclerk generally in charge. It has been well said the best golfer is a complete moron for if he thinks, the game has so much tension he is going to take an eight on a par four last hole where a five would have won him a championship. Just to bear out this thesis, think if any of the great golfers ever wrote a book until the day of the ghost writers came along.

Wulla was a really fine golfer and many took lessons, but to the best of my belief he never used more than seven words for his instruction. If a bad shot was made he said, "You didna' hit the ba'." If a good shot, "Gude shot." But some of the younger generation learned a bit by observation and imitation and golf began to come into its own.

Some outstanding golfers have learned their game over these hills, such as Sam Snead, and in the amateur ranks Ellis Knowles, now the perennial winner of the Veterans Championship and for years a threat in the National Amateur. One of the finest, though his career was cut short, was Adam Green, a long, gangling mountaineer, but how he could hit the ball! He graduated to the position of pro from the rank of caddies after Park left. Those who saw Adam in his prime still maintain that none of the present-day long hitters could have touched him, just as no one has ever punched like John L. Sullivan. In the course of time Adam took unto himself a wife from the State of Maine, who became quite a character. Her first entry to the hall of fame came when someone offered her lobster at a function. "Not for me. I came from Maine where the lobsters grow and if they came by train I know how long it took them to get here."

In the course of time Adam's wife became cashier at the club house. It did not take long for her tongue to become famous and many tried to get a "rise" out of her, usually to their discomfiture. One guest, who still comes to The Homestead, met her walking out before closing time and in the presence of a number of bystanders called to her: "Mrs. Green, aren't you knocking off ahead of time? How long have you been quitting before the job is done?" Ma Green that day was wearing a pair of bright blue stockings to match her hair and, without batting an eye, replied, "Ever since you gave me these blue stockings." That finished the banter.

Eventually Adam's eyes began to stray and one day we heard he had departed for the mines in West Virginia in the company of two ladies of color. Ma Green carried on as before and no one raised the subject with her. A few years later, when there was the usual ten o'clock crowd in the golf room, the telephone rang. Ma Green answered it in a voice all could hear. "Yes, Mr. Bobbitt." Bobbitt was at that time the Express agent at Hot Springs. A moment's silence while Bobbitt spoke, and then Ma Green went on: "You say you've got Adam down there in a pine box? All right, you have work to do; so have I. Go on about your business and I will about mine. When I get these people started I'll take care of Adam but I don't want to be bothered now." The players waiting to get balls, sign tickets and the like, were somewhat upset but Ma Green went right ahead with her work as if nothing had happened, and later in the day went to the station and "took care of Adam."

The little six-hole course proved to be a hardy and vigorous plant and began to grow almost as soon as the first player completed a round, for a long time without much direction, extending out along the lines of least resistance where there was already cleared land. The first plunge into woodland came when the present third hole was cleared. The early guidance was completely amateur and by cut and try methods. Donald Ross was called in eventually and from that visit there came an eighteen-hole course. Ross did not have much of a chance for in those days the idea of grading or applying engineering to golf courses was in its infancy. Peter Lee made some changes and there was always experimenting going on. It was not until 1924, after Flynn had made a success of the Cascades course, that a comprehensive plan was finally worked out and the one then adopted, with minor changes, represents the present layout.

During these years of growth many interesting and amusing holes were tried. There had always existed upland pasture land where the "Goat Course," now maintained for employees, is and, as the easiest way, some of this was utilized. One hole, which is still in use as the second hole of the Goat Course, was about 130 yards long, going up the precipitous bank by the seventeenth green, with the putting green on the floor of a sinkhole, a real crater hole out of sight up the hill. While this was in use Bob Wrenn, one of America's greatest sportsmen, was playing and being bothered by a pair of Tammany politicians who kept driving into him and his partner. Bob was putting on this hole when one and then another ball came soaring over the rim of the crater. He picked the balls up and deposited one in the hole and the other about an inch away, as if it had struck the flag and bounced off. Holes in one were even more infrequent then than now and that night there wasn't a person in Hot Springs who did not have all the champagne he wanted, at the expense of Tammany Hall.

The Homestead course for many years had one true distinction, an actual, not a figurative, nineteenth hole. The eighteenth green was at the teeing ground on the present practice fairway. There were no tennis courts beyond the creek and the practice putting green, a one-hole affair, was where it is now. It was a mashie shot from the eighteenth green to the practice putting green and on the finish of a match the caddies were sent scurrying ahead to clear away the putters so the question of payment for caddies and drinks could be settled playing the nineteenth hole.

Most of the holes, until Flynn's final revisions, would have suited the King of France who marched up the hill and then marched down again. One, the tenth I believe, had a green, now utilized for the grass garden, just below the present eleventh tee. The tee was on the hillside above where pines have since been planted. The hole was 180 yards long and in summer when the course dried out you could use either a midiron and hit the ball hard to carry the green or tap it off the tee with a putter and have it roll down to it. One method was as effective as the other; the ball would end up in about the same place in any event. Another, which gave a thrill to long hitters, was the eighth, where the tee was up in the pines above the present ninth tee, crossing the present ninth green midway and then down the lane still left through the trees to the highway. It was 380 yards long with the crest of the hill about 200 yards from the tee, and a ball that got over the crest would roll on down to the green for a record distance.

First and last there was some fine golf played over the Homestead course. Two of the best rounds were played by Glenna Collett and Helen Hicks in the finals of one of the Women's Fall Tournaments. Both girls had 72's over the course substantially as it is now and, at that, halved the seventh hole in a mighty seven. This particular match was full of thrills, including the finish when Glenna missed her drive on the twentieth hole and won by holing a chip. She also managed to halve the sixteenth by a most extraordinary shot. She was to the right on her drive and the ball lay between some tree roots. After long study she took a tremendous swing.

The ball went out, bounced through the bunker and stopped two feet from the pin. The gallery went wild, but the referee who happened to be standing by her as she hit the ball saw that she almost missed it, just nicking the top, which bounced it out, the only way it could have been extricated from the roots.

Golf was certainly different in the days of the gutta ball and I am far from sure it was not a better game. To play, one had to be able to use the tools of the trade with real skill. There was no specializing and a putter, lofter, cleek and driver, with perhaps a baffy, made up a full kit of clubs. The player had to accomplish the variety of shots which are still called for by careful manipulation rather than by the use of different instruments. But it was a nuisance, if playing an important match, to have to take a second caddy along to carry a bucket of ice water to keep the gutta balls hard enough not to get out of shape.

When Peter Lee was called in sometime early in the twentieth century, one of the mistakes similar to that of building the Virginia Hotel was perpetrated on golf. Already one course was proving inadequate. Lee did not believe in or know much about engineering but trusted, for distances, to guesswork and the length of his stride, simply ignoring elevations. He conceived the idea of extending the Goat Course along the side of the mountain, and designed a layout which went south, coming down the hollow at the first turn of the Delafield road and almost to the Catholic Church. It all looked beautiful on paper and large sums were spent on clearing land and preparation for seeding. My brother, George, and I were the only members of the family who knew much of golf and we were only able to come to Hot Springs at rather rare intervals. We turned up for one of the September sixth events and were shown what had been done. The engineer had checked elevations with no instrument but a small pocket altimeter, which later proved to have been inaccurate. One walk and George and I killed the project. Now the only trace of it is one of the greens on the Goat Course and the fact that the trees on the south side of the Delafield road, from Woodland Cottage to the first hairpin turn, are second growth. When people ask how long it will take to reforest burnt or cut over areas in these mountains I like to show them this place where there was no artificial planting and in thirty years or so, quite a respectable young forest has come in.

For fifty years the Homestead course has been a laboratory for growing and maintaining grass on a golf course. The Virginia Hot Springs Golf and Tennis Club was one of the first member clubs of the United States Golf Association and is still a going organization, with certain proprietary rights in the course and an arrangement with the hotel for play by Homestead guests. It has worked closely with the Green Section of the United States Golf Association, and many new developments at the Arlington Experiment Station of the United States Department of Agriculture have been tried out here under actual playing conditions. Often players have found fairways marked off in lanes, which meant that different methods of fertilization, watering, cutting or seeding were being tried. At one time one of the greens was planted in pie-shaped sections with a different strain of bent in each. These experiments were not always successful. Strangely enough one of the unsolved problems of a fine golf course at Hot Springs is to prevent vigorous growth of grass where it isn't wanted. In this natural bluegrass country the rough will grow too tough. If it is mown down, it simply gets thicker and if something like a fescue is planted, it is only a year or two before it is

choked out by bluegrass. We have tried to check the
growth in the rough by almost every method. Chemicals
kill it but next year the bluegrass is back worse than ever.
The only partial solution is to scrape off the topsoil for
five or six inches and sow a thin growing grass on what
should be sterile clay, but even that does not seem to be
always successful.

One of the first of these experiments was made early
in the twenties. The Green Section had sent us a piece
of sod some years before and either failed to give adequate
instructions concerning it or they were overlooked. It
was thrown on a refuse heap where it grew and some
years later we learned it was a sample of the first vegetative
strain of bent to be developed. When this was recognized
it was shredded and planted on the fifteenth green. In
the meantime the Green Section had mislaid the records
of what was sent. This grass thrived from the start. It
is practically indistinguishable from Metropolitan Bent
unless growing side by side. It has proven to be the best
for our climate and soil and has been propagated in our
grass garden and is gradually supplanting all other
strains on both courses.

The lack of knowledge of grass growing in the early
days is well shown by an embarrassing experience of one
of our chief engineers. I had begun to learn about the
merits of the bent grasses and wanted bent sown in the
fairways. This engineer maintained there was something
about our climate that made it impossible to grow bent.
Dr. Piper, then head of the Green Section, came down
and I told him my troubles. We went for a walk on the
course in company with the engineer. Piper soon stopped
and had the engineer explain at length why bent could
not be grown. Then, stooping down, he plucked a handful

of grass and remarked, "Mr. X, you have made a great discovery. You have convinced me that bent will not thrive here, yet this grass looks to me exactly like bent." He then took out a pocket magnifying glass and examined the grass carefully. "Exactly like bent in all its desirable qualities and yet grows wild where bent will not. This is new to me and may revolutionize the maintenance of golf courses." Nothing more was said but a few days later the engineer sheepishly handed me a requisition for bent seed.

Of the many schemes for fertilizing, watering, methods of cutting and the like which have had their rise and fall in the science of agronomy as applied to golf courses, there are few which have not been tried here. The latest, which seems to promise much, is the control of weeds by chemical treatment.

If there were many great golfers who learned the game playing the Homestead course, all who played it did not go around in par. One of the most enthusiastic in the twenties, Frank B. Kellogg, whose greatness lay in other fields than golf, came to Hot Springs first when Senator, and often later when Secretary of State. Now, with improved road surface and many by-passes, it takes smart driving to come from Washington to Hot Springs in four and a half hours, and yet many times I took the telephone off the hook around nine o'clock to hear— "This is Frank Kellogg. I am bringing down a friend and will meet you on the first tee at one-thirty." And there he would be, no fussier than usual, and "raring" to go. The friend usually turned out to be a par or sub-par player and I was expected to provide a fourth to make an even match. Mr. Kellogg wanted to win but didn't care who carried the burden, himself or his partner. Perhaps he was trained by experience in seeking international cooperation.

Mr. Kellogg had a fine contempt for any rules of golf which did not suit his game. I remember his delight when one day we had Nick Longworth along and Nick announced at the first tee, "Well, we'll play winter rules, and liberally interpreted too." That just suited Mr. Kellogg, who felt it was only just that if his ball lodged near the whitewashed plank fence which in those days marked the course off from the highway, he should toss it out where he could swing, and if the toss did not come to rest in a good lie, then why not two tosses?

One of these games was a triumph for me in other than a golfing sense. Chief Justice Hughes and one of Kellogg's golfing diplomats made up the foursome. I was playing with the Chief Justice and having a hard time holding up our side. The Chief Justice was more meticulous but not as skillful as the Secretary and we were getting beaten. At last there came a hole where Mr. Hughes had a chance to win a point and square the match. He foozled and turning to me said, "It's just no use. I'm going to quit trying and you save what you can." Then I took a chance: "Mr. Hughes," I said, "I'm going to play super golf and we'll win; but, win or lose, this is the happiest moment of my life. I'm even with you. I served my apprenticeship under Jimmie Byrne, a friend and admirer of yours but the hardest taskmaster a young man ever knew. Many times in the wee sma' hours of the night, tired from days and nights of frantic work, I would want to let down, to have Byrne push the papers aside, take off his piece-nez, and carefully laying them aside say, 'Ingalls, I'm disappointed in you. How do you think you can ever become a lawyer?

Do you think Mr. Hughes was ever willing to quit?'
Now I can feel you are really human after all."

The Justice looked blank for a moment, then laughed.
I confess I did not make good and we lost that day,
but we had many pleasant games thereafter and I came
to have a real affection for a kindly, generous and tolerant
gentleman, in spite of the beard and ramrod back.

One figure no one who played golf from the earliest
days will ever forget was Colonel Edward Colston. The
Colonel had lost his left arm in a skirmish a few days
after Lee's surrender, but that never daunted him in anything, let alone golf. With one arm, learning the game
long after middle age, he developed a truly classic swing
and could often get good distance. His putting and shots
from difficult lies were something else.

Colonel Colston had his roots deeply in Hot Springs.
During the Civil War he was at the Healing Springs Hotel
for a time when it was used as a hospital, recovering from
a wound. Another time he had his first swim at Hot
Springs. He was leading his regiment through the Valley
after a trying and exhausting campaign of fighting and
marching over hot and dusty roads. The column straggled
into Hot Springs, dirty and bedraggled. As the men saw
the Hot Springs pools they broke ranks and ran for the
water. The Colonel himself was worn out and for two
days let discipline go to the winds while all, men and
officers, luxuriated in the warm waters.

The Colonel's connection with Hot Springs went
even farther back than the Civil War, one of his ancestors being the Dr. John Brockenbrough who owned
Warm Springs from 1828 to 1852. His case was like
that of a man once employed as an upholsterer in The
Homestead who, being asked when he learned his trade.

said "In 1809." That seemed a bit odd but it turned out his great-grandfather had been an upholsterer at the Viennese Court, so he was born with the trade.

Whether it was atavism, memories of the Civil War, or just because he loved the Valley, Colonel Colston constantly returned with his family, finally dying in The Homestead. He first stayed at Midway Inn, between the Hot and the Healing, and, after that burned, for many years had one of the original Homestead cottages. There was always ready in that cottage a super mint julep and often a gay poker party, presided over by Aunt Polly, of sparkling wit, the Colonel's second wife. He married her when his first wife, her sister, died and she brought up his two children.

The Colonel was a prominent lawyer from Cincinnati, a good raconteur and a delightful gentleman. He never forgot the commanding tones and sulphurous language learned as a cavalry commander and, in consequence, could be easily found on the golf links. To the end he remained an unregenerate rebel. When on his deathbed he sent for his physician and greeted him with, "I'm going to die this time and I want to say something first." This was a bit gruesome to the physician, who tried to calm him down to no avail. "When I die someone is going to have to sign my death certificate and that will be you, won't it?" Again the doctor tried to turn the conversation but the Colonel went on, "In this death certificate you have to put where I was born?" The doctor nodded. "All right. I was born in Charlestown, Virginia and if you or any other S. O. B. writes down West Virginia I'll come back and haunt him for the rest of his days!" He died a few hours later.

# 20. *The Cascades Golf Course*

IN SPITE of all the work on the Homestead golf course
it was inadequate and unsatisfactory. The need
for an additional course had been recognized early
and the unfortunate experiment with Peter Lee had
failed. The course was short, too much up and down hill,
and the holes were not laid out in accordance with modern
demands. Many of its shortcomings have been subsequently overcome but its inadequacy to provide room
for play never could have been remedied.

For a long time the idea was toyed with of a course to be built on the land owned by the Warrens, midway between the Hot and the Healing. However, it would have been difficult to build a really top course on that terrain; it did not have particular scenic attraction and, most of all, there was the water question. The attractive feature was nearness to The Homestead. The deciding adverse factor, however, was the exorbitant price the owners asked for the land.

The thought of the Rubino land, the old "Little Healing," was constantly in mind and Raynor, a well-known golf architect, was asked to make a survey to see if a course could be built there, although at that time the property could not be purchased. His adverse report is understandable for his survey did not take into consideration the possibility of acquiring the Thompson Farm also, on which most of the fifth, sixth, seventh, eighth and ninth fairways lie. Without this there was not enough land.

The crowding of the Homestead course got worse as time went on and when in 1923 the chance came to buy the Rubino property, the genesis of the Cascades course occurred. The history of the Rubino property is interesting and explains many things, such as the rather unusual club house.

There is a strange geological phenomenon at Healing Springs. The spring under the small canopy in the grounds of the Inn, which is *the* Healing Springs, giving the place its name, is at an elevation of 2,100 feet above sea level. Going south, Route 220 crosses a limestone ridge about 400 yards from the Inn and the cut through which the highway passes is at an altitude of 2,263 feet. This ridge is a spur running west off the Warm Springs Mountain to a point perhaps a half mile from where the highway crosses it. The ridge divides the break in Little Mountain, called the Healing Springs Gap, in two parts, with the drainage from Healing Springs flowing west along the north side of this ridge and the Cascades stream, also flowing west but along the south side, joining below the last waterfall. Route 220 descends, after crossing Sawmill Ridge, to the Cascades Club. A little north of the seventeenth green is a spring, now housed over and piped into the creek in the first pool. The extraordinary thing is that this spring at the Cascades and the one at the Healing are as nearly alike as human measurement can determine. They are both thermal springs, that being a more or less technical term to denote a spring the temperature of which differs from the usual springs in a given area, indicating that its waters come from great depths. Not only is the temperature of these two springs identical but, so far as that could be determined when it was a material factor in a lawsuit, they have the same chemical analysis. They break forth at approximately the same level. The flow of neither has been accurately measured to my knowledge but from observation they seem to be the same. Thinking back over the definition of thermal springs it seems strange how the main source, which must feed both of these, has bifurcated below the level of the limestone strata and both branches found equal passages through the clay and detritus of the old valley floor.

The similarity of these two springs was recognized at a very early date and in the records of Healing Springs we have two place names—Healing Springs, which is now the Cascades Inn, and the "Little Healing," which is the Cascades Club. This may sound like a digression but it is because of it that the Cascades Club was built where it is, and it is this fact which determined the rather weird architecture of the Club and which delayed the acquisition of the Cascades property for many years.

I have mentioned meeting Jakey Rubino when I first came to the Healing as a child. The Healing Springs waters were at that time reputed to be specifics for the social diseases, much as those of Hot Springs, Arkansas, have been. Jakey had many Broadway friends who were interested in such waters. Fortunately, or unfortunately, depending on the point of view, when the Virginia Hot Springs Company acquired the Healing it was determined that the business which might be attracted by a cure of such diseases would not be desirable. This decision was supported by scepticism as to the efficacy of the cure.

Rubino knew of the similarity of the two springs and in 1895 bought the Little Healing. In the meantime quite a trade had been developed in the sale of Healing Springs Water, not for the purpose for which the springs were famous but as a drinking water. Actually it was a hard, flat water and bad medicine for the digestive apparatus. However, there was a demand for it and people did not know as much about mineral waters as they do now. As soon as Rubino got the Little Healing he began to market the water as "Rubino Healing Springs Water" and litigation was commenced to enjoin his use of the words "Healing Springs." This was long and costly and Rubino finally won but by that time the world had changed and no one bothered with the business. The only relic of the mineral water business now is one of the dormitories for maids at the Inn, which is the old bottling house remodeled.

Rubino was at that time a successful floor trader on the New York Stock Exchange. He was used extensively by J. B. Haggin in his market operations and for a long while rode high, wide and handsome. Rubino began at once an extensive development of the property. As his residence he erected the building now used as the Club House. The design before it was modified was something fearful and wonderful to behold. Coming in the front door there was the present little entrance hall and just beyond was a swimming pool filled with Little Healing Springs water; around its margin were beautifully tiled dressing rooms. For years after this was all torn out tons of the tile were used by the Company for tiled showers in the employees' locker rooms and the like. Upstairs Rubino's own personal room was the one just beyond the dining room. His Chick Sale was out of doors on the small balcony off this room. The other rooms upstairs were for his guests.

Rubino added other buildings, a small power plant, a superintendent's brick house which used to stand in the middle of the first fairway, and the magnificent stable, which the Company last year remodeled, with apartments on the second floor and shops for the golf course on the first. A bit more vision when the course was built would have taken this stable for the Club House.

The place completed, with a cress lake where the seventeenth fairway now lies, Rubino proceeded to entertain lavishly. There were trout in the stream and game down the gap. Perhaps champagne was not indigenous, but when the course was built ten two-ton truck loads of broken fizzy water bottles were removed from the site of the tenth tee.

This life went on for a time but inevitably there came a day of reckoning. The attempt to corner the stock of the National Cordage Company blew up and Rubino was wiped out. He was indebted to Haggin for immense sums and in settlement deeded to him the Little

Healing, together with coal lands and other property. It was only a short time after this that Rubino died and his heirs brought suit against Haggin to have the deed construed as a mortgage, not as satisfaction of a debt. The suit was not prosecuted vigorously but in the meantime it tied up the title and not until the statute of limitations had expired could the Haggins dispose of the property.

One day in 1923 Allen McCulloch, attorney for the Haggins, called me by phone from New York and said that at last the Haggins were in a position to sell. He had promised the refusal of the property to the Company and said he now had another customer but if the Company wanted it at the price asked, which was a fair one, it could be bought though the deal had to be closed before the end of that week.

Quick action was necessary and the long-distance telephone was worked overtime. The board of directors of the Company authorized the purchase *if* a competent golf architect would give assurance that a satisfactory course could be built.

The next problem was to get the golf architect. Several of national reputation could not come immediately and more or less by accident the name of William S. Flynn was suggested. Flynn had up to then built no outstanding courses but had worked on Pine Valley and the Philadelphia Cricket Club. The reports were that he was honest, thoroughly understood golf, was not hidebound by convention, and that what he had done not only gave good golf but took unusual advantage of landscaping possibilities. All of this proved to be the case.

Flynn came to Hot Springs and by that time we had just one day to settle the matter. It was a steaming hot August day. Flynn was not very tall but was almost

as wide as high and full of energy. Except for time off
while getting an option on the Thompson farm, I dogged
his footsteps from arrival until dark. The flat around the
Club House was in corn and the seventeenth fairway a
water-cress lake. That was not so bad although everything was weedy and brushy, the heat stifling and the
thought of snakes hiding under bushes always present.
However, he was not satisfied with going over only the
cleared land. We had a surveyor checking elevations and
pushed through the woods where the second and third
fairways are now located, then down a wild, rock-filled
ravine to the fourth green and through a perfect tangle '
of briers and boulders by the tenth green, along the
eleventh, twelfth and thirteenth fairways.

The hotter and more tired I got the more I wanted
to find out what Flynn thought, but he gave not the
slightest indication. At dusk we washed some of the dust
and grime out of our throats with good Scotch, and Flynn
took a sheet of foolscap and made some figures. Studying these for a time he said, "If you can get the piece
on which that negro shack stands I have twenty locations
where I can put a putting green. I don't know how the
holes will run but if I have two extra sites for greens I
can build you a course. It is going to cost money and take
engineering but I believe you will have an outstanding
course and certainly one of the most beautiful anywhere."

That was all there was to it. The next day the deal
was closed with McCulloch. A chance was taken on
getting the Watkins lot as it was first supposed he was
just a squatter, and in the end he got a price per acre
for the site of the fourth green which if it had applied
to the rest of the property would have made the Cascades the most costly land for a golf course in the world.
The Rubino property comprised 1,702 acres, the Thomp-

son farm 242 acres and Watkins' lot one-fourth of an acre.

That was not the end of land purchases however. The Cascades spring is the finest and largest source of water in the Valley for miles. Almost before work was started on the course the idea occurred that it would be valuable as water supply to supplement that derived from the springs on Warm Springs Mountain. Actually since its acquisition there have been at least three years when, without the Cascades water, The Homestead and Hot Springs would have been almost out of business for several months at a time. Unfortunately, the stream, after leaving the Rubino property, flowed for a short distance across the Barney Johnson farm, then owned by Bernard Northern, who had a grist mill just before the stream joined that flowing from Hot Springs. Notice was served on the Company that injunction proceedings would be started at once to bar diversion of water from the Cascades to another watershed, and in the end the whole Johnson farm of 1,280 acres was purchased to get about three hundred yards of stream. Perhaps it is as well the purchase was made, for this end of the stream is now of importance to trout fishing and the farm itself, first used as a vegetable garden, has lately been valuable to round out farming operations.

Once the property was acquired, construction of the course was pushed as rapidly as possible. There were many tricky problems met and conquered. One of the worst was the existence of Swift Run, rising south of the sixth fairway and running through the course to below the thirteenth green. Most of the water which used to run down it now goes in pipes to Hot Springs but, draining a wide territory, it is still subject to heavy floods. For more than half the distance the course of the stream had to be shifted and for about a hundred yards on the sixth fairway, where it was impossible to get sufficient width, it was bridged. This bridging was done by laying locust logs on stone abutments with a span of about forty feet, then covering the logs with topsoil and growing grass on that. In 1946 the stone abutments began to give way and the bridging was replaced with a six-foot steel culvert. The amazing thing about this is that when the locust logs were taken up, except for a few feet on each end they were found to be as sound as ever. The stream was also carried in culverts by the fifth and tenth greens. Perhaps the worst difficulty was in getting the twelfth and thirteenth fairways established. The twelfth was crossed by a hard limestone ridge about three hundred yards from the tee and both were a mass of boulders. The cress lake on the seventeenth was another problem never entirely solved in spite of a network of drainage. It would have been better if the bull had been taken by the horns and the stream channel deepened instead of trying to fill in the lake.

Flynn's original layout has of course been greatly modified. Until his death all changes were under his supervision, the last of these being moving the first green back about fifty yards to its present position. Practically every green, first and last, has been rebuilt. Flynn's plans were never those of a construction engineer and he expected modifications as the work progressed. One of his general directions was "Slopes on greens never more than one in thirty." The engineer in charge was not a golfer and, instead of taking this as an allowable maximum in case of necessity, thought he could use the figures wherever convenient. Until many greens were rebuilt, putting on the Cascades was an experience. Naturally, in the beginning the grass was not thick and, with steep slopes, anything might and did happen. Ultimately the first, third, sixth, ninth, tenth, eleventh, twelfth, thirteenth, fifteenth and seventeenth greens were completely rebuilt, some on the same location and others near by.

Climbing on the Cascades is considerably less than on the Homestead—in fact, the first hole and last ten are practically level. However, the course is really on two levels. At least once this afforded an opportunity for a bit of spite work on the part of some members of the Press. The Women's National Golf Championship was played here in 1925, during the last week of September. There were a large number of newswriters present and a tent was put up by the first tee to give them a place to work. As happens at times there was a cold snap, with temperatures hovering around freezing and quite a breeze. The tent was pretty cold, it must be admitted, and the newswriters put out; they thought the gals and gallery ought to have been evicted from the Club House for their benefit. But they got even. They went to the foot of the hill below the ninth tee and, as the large gallery filed down the steps, pointed their cameras upward, and then distributed the resulting picture all over the country with the caption "Some of the hills the girls had to climb over at Hot Springs."

The first ball was driven on the Cascades in October of 1924. The course has since been the scene of many tournaments, the Women's National and the Intercollegiate the only ones of national importance. B. F. Jones, of Pittsburgh, was an ardent admirer of golf, although by the time the Cascades was opened he had ceased to play. He gave a cup which he named "The Fairacre Cup" after his house at Hot Springs, and The Fairacre was the first tournament over the Cascades.

The cup has been won outright once, to be replaced by George Warrington, and the play for it is an annual event starting the week before and finishing on Labor Day. It brings out the best golf in Virginia, even better than the State Championship, also frequently played here, and the chief trouble with it is too many entries.

# 21. *Illegal Activities Along the Road*

THE PROBLEM of obtaining liquid refreshment brings up the question of "moonshining" which I find is always a matter of curiosity to visitors to the Valley. The whiskey for which the selling price was fixed at the 1791 term of court was undoubtedly distilled locally and from then on a considerable proportion of the corn raised on the mountain farms was marketed in liquid form. In fact the word "corn" without qualification, particularly in the days of prohibition, was a synonym for corn whiskey. This use of the word produced some red faces for the revenue agents on the occasion of one of the early community suppers for the benefit of the Visiting Nurse Association. Tom Sterrett, who for so many years was treasurer of the Association and general factotum for all business, was supervising the arrangements for the supper. The mainstay of these suppers was always fried chicken and roasting ears. That year we had a late spring and no local corn was ripe. Tom learned that over on the Cowpasture River, at a lower altitude, a farmer had roasting ears. While standing around the post office gossiping, one of his friends asked what was to be done for corn and Tom told him about the farmer on the river. The farm was off the beaten road and Tom explained that he was having difficulty getting a truck to make the trip and bring the corn over. A prohibition officer was standing by and, unfortunately for him, put two and two together to make five—a load of corn over the mountain, and difficulty in getting a truck which would make the trip. That sounded as if it meant a load of liquor, with the trucker afraid of being caught for illegal transportation. The agent also heard the name of the owner of the truck, who happened to have been suspected of using it for the profitable if dangerous business of bringing in moonshine. He also heard that the truck could only get in late the night before the supper.

The night came and it was a cold, rainy one. It was well, when interfering with moonshiners, to go in sufficient force to discourage resistance. Liquor had been moving quite freely and the enforcement officers thought this was a chance for a big haul. They took a large posse and hid in the bushes by a bend of the road. There was no shelter and it got colder and clammier every moment but they stuck to their vigil. Long past midnight they heard the rumble of the truck coming up the mountain and as it rounded the turn the posse met it, with rifles pointed at the driver, a regular Wild West hold-up. The poor driver was astonished, to say the least, but he respected the authority of the guns. They hauled him off the seat, slipped handcuffs on him, and proceeded to search the truck for the "corn." All sorts of bribes were offered to the driver to keep the story quiet, but it was too good to kill.

Even in its heyday moonshining was, as a rule, carried on in remote districts. The hazards of the trade were greater in transporting to the ultimate customer than in the manufacture. As stills were off the beaten track and the approach of revenue officers easily detected in advance, revenuers were loath to face the perils of a raid. On the other hand, the highways could be watched and a "pinch" involved less peril to the officers. In consequence it became the rule to "go and get it if you wanted it."

This situation resulted in a harrowing night for three residents of the county. The story got around that a man in Augusta County had a supply of excellent, aged corn. Quite a few people wanted a share. Ultimately Carl Hillman, Chris Andersen and one of the medical fraternity offered to make the trip—all being prominent citizens, they felt there was little probability of their being stopped by casual enforcement officers. They left Hot Springs early in the afternoon on a gray November day and it was getting toward dusk when they found the still, made their trade and loaded up to return. This and that friend of the trio had handed them commissions so, with their own supplies, they had about all the car would hold.

All went well until it began to sleet. The road beyond Warm Springs was unpaved for thirty-five miles and, with no defroster or windshield wiper, progress was slow and driving tricky. About seven o'clock and five miles north of Goshen, Hillman, who was driving, missed a rut and they slithered gently down into the ditch. It was pitch dark. They did not dare hail a passing car for help—in fact, the last thing they wanted was for an unknown passer-by to stop. Car lights were put out and they scrunched down amid the jugs when any vehicle came by, so it would look like a deserted car. There they spent the whole night, miserable, cold and wet. Next morning at daybreak one of the trio waded several miles through the mud to the home of a farmer he knew, and found him feeding his stock. For a small commission on the cargo the farmer took a horse and log chain to the stalled car and got them on their way. They were a bedraggled lot when they arrived at Hot Springs, fortunately with no further misadventure.

As was inevitable during prohibition, I had quite a few personal contacts with the moonshine fraternity. If their "corn" was sufficiently aged and the man knew his business the resulting drink was pretty good, it was certainly better than most of the Scotch and other ersatz liquor which city dwellers consumed. There was one man, operating within ten miles of The Homestead, who claimed to make superlative whiskey. He attributed the excellence of his product to his manner of aging it. A small stream flowed through his place, not a real brook, little more than a wet weather drain although the stream bed, in shale, was always damp. He used to put his liquor in casks and bury it in the stream bed. This made it difficult for the Revenue officers to find the hiding place and, as the wooden cask was continually moist, he did not have to worry about evaporation.

My earliest meeting with moonshiners came when I was quite a kid. This was long before the days of prohibition and the moonshining just to avoid the tax. We were on a fishing trip and driving by night. Taking a back road we heard a shot and a few minutes later overtook a man carrying a gun. We were perhaps four hundred yards from a farmhouse and could see a fire in the yard, like one built under a soap kettle. Midnight seemed a strange time to make soap and perhaps we were a bit too inquisitive. Anyway, we were invited politely enough, at the point of a Winchester, to come up to the house and explain ourselves. Our story seemed to be acceptable and we had sense enough to take a nip of the raw brew as it flowed from the still. The idea was that if we took that drink we became *particeps criminis* to the operation and could not give evidence against the gang. Much later, studying law, I wondered about the soundness of this doctrine, but it was thoroughly believed by the moonshiners and got us off without trouble that time. Anyway, directly from the still, the Indians were right in calling whiskey firewater. Once again, when I fell off Natural Bridge on a cold day and got a thorough ducking, a good Samaritan offered me a glass of what looked like aqua pura but which, if not distilled that morning, was not many days old. It certainly warmed me up.

My pleasantest experiences with the moonshiners, however, had nothing to do with their operations. Wandering about the headwaters of Anthony's Creek in Pocahontas County, West Virginia, while grouse shooting, I saw some hollows that looked inviting. The land was owned by a lumber company which long before had ceased operations but, as usual, I stopped at a cabin at the mouth of the hollow and asked about going up, although knowing the cabin owner had no more right to the hollow than I. At first, only the woman of the house was there and she tried to dissuade me, saying too many hunters had shot her tame turkeys, but I hung around and when the man of the house came along managed to establish friendly relations. In the end he agreed that I might go, with the single proviso that I carry a few buckshot loads and kill any bear I might meet, as they had been killing his sheep. I didn't meet a bear although I saw a number of carcasses, where sheep had been killed. I got some fine shooting but the most remarkable part of the whole thing was the way those people knew where I was. I walked slowly up the hollow while my dog ranged on ahead. After some two or three miles I came on a man sitting at the mouth of an entering hollow. He was obviously expecting me and knew all about me. How the information got there ahead of me I never could figure out. This man told me where to look for birds and the advice was good. He also warned me not to go into certain hollows as "there are no pheasants in them." I never questioned this but later on, when I got to know the people better, I was taken up some of these forbidden areas, where I found birds and also other things.

These West Virginians were, I suppose, true moonshiners. I never met anything but courtesy and kindness from them. Their little farms were pitiful affairs, with scrawny cattle grubbing around in rocky pastures. I have no doubt that for generations the sale of moonshine had made life possible.

Today these moonshiners are gone or reformed and the woods are part of a national forest, protected by forest rangers and game wardens. Roads are better and the largest cars can get to the hollows which used to have so many birds. Instead of birds, there are camps of hunters befouling the woods with tin cans, bottles and litter. I cannot help but wonder whether there was not more honest, straightforward living in the old, illicit days than there is now in a well policed and managed forest.

Prohibition, which came to Virginia before the rest of the country, created some problems for visitors to The Homestead, particularly in the Japanese Room, then at the peak of its glory. The worst difficulty to be met was that if people brought their liquor with them, packed in their trunks, the trains ran from Staunton to Clifton Forge in the middle of the night without a stop and somehow as they dashed through tunnels and around curves it all disappeared, sometimes only temporarily. George McFadden came down once, with two cases of champagne on leaving Philadelphia and none on arrival. That was not the sort of loss George could stand. He conferred with Shep, who assured him that by the next night he could get him some champagne which would certainly be satisfactory. The champagne came and was poured from a napkin-covered bottle. George remarked that it was good and asked Shep to let him see the bottle. "How much will this cost me?" he asked. Shep told him. "It ought to be good. I thought it was when I bought it in Philadelphia and I am paying just twice as much again at Hot Springs. The cost of transportation is certainly high." Shep never did explain how that champagne made the last lap of its journey.

## 22. *Horses and Hounds*

PEOPLE have often been amazed that there was at Hot Springs for a long period a Hunt, recognized by the Master of Fox Hounds Association, with all the formality consequent thereto. This came about as a result of the background of love of horses and hunting which my wife and I had.

We have been fond of horses for as long as either can remember. Her first recollection is of a birthday present of a pony when she was four years old, and one of my most vivid memories is of my pony, May, which

I had when we lived at White Sulphur. I had a riding horse while at the law school and Rachel had one until we were married. There was no place in the budget of a struggling young lawyer for horses and there followed a long hiatus in horse interests for both of us. Later on when we built a quite large house on Long Island Rachel was busy with babies and I with a host of other matters so, except for a pony for the children, horses passed out of our orbit until we came to Hot Springs in 1922.

On getting to Virginia horses again became a major interest. For two years we lived in The Homestead, then for a year rented the French house. During that time we used horses from the Homestead Livery for riding and driving, but in 1925 we put the money from the sale of our Long Island house into The Yard at Hot Springs and at the same time built a stable appurtenant to the house. The next year we bought Hobby Horse Farm, Rachel bought a stallion and some brood mares, and we were in the horse business. It was not long before Rachel got a hunter. She had followed the hounds as a young girl and now began to visit the Warrenton country and hunt there. I went along but was never a bona fide pink coat individual. As everyone does, I had plenty of falls. Perhaps I lost my nerve but claim that fundamentally I had more than many of my friends who were afraid to admit that from the top of a horse the ground looked a long way off. The damn beasts have a way of doing the unexpected, such as falling down themselves, bolting through forests, or simply jumping one off.

The words "fox hunting" are magic to any Virginian, whether in the fashionable Piedmont, the lowlands of Eastern Virginia or in the mountains. Mountain fox

hunting has its charm and, be it remembered, its conventions, different from those of organized packs with
hunt liveries and pink coats, but equally sophisticated in
its way. Tate Sterrett had a pack one time at Fassifern
and, until the game laws made it a serious offense if
hounds got away and ran deer, almost every farmer kept
one or two hounds which would run a fox or a coon.
Mostly these mountain hunts take place at night. Even
today, if one will go but a short distance off the paved
highway, on a frosty moonlit night the sound of hounds
giving tongue on the chase will be heard. The owners of
the hounds seldom are mounted but follow on foot as
well as possible, seeking a hill or other vantage point
from which to listen to the music or for a glimpse of the
quarry. This works out pretty well as most of our foxes
are grays, which circle.

We had not been in Hot Springs long when it became
noised around that we were enthusiastic hunters, and
we went out many times both for foxes and coons.

From these modest beginnings Rachel reached out
for more elaborate sport and set about establishing a real
pack of hounds and a formal Hunt. Cecil Tuke was then
manager of the Homestead Stables and she arranged for
him and Addison Gutschall, one of the riding masters, to
act as whips. She accumulated hounds, getting the first
from Jackson Boyd, then Master of the Moore County
Hounds, at Southern Pines, North Carolina. Others were
obtained by gift and purchase from sundry packs where
she had hunted, and these hounds were kenneled at The
Yard. At one time she had a pack which consisted of
about twenty-five couple.

While sympathetic to the idea of a Hunt, except in
the very beginning I was seldom in the field. As a matter
of fact, as it developed I did less and less riding for in-

stead of the casual wandering over new and old paths I found, as we got more horses, that the only animal for me to ride became a colt that had to be schooled or a hunter which needed a workout.

The Hunt was Rachel's personal venture and only because of her enthusiasm and hard work was success attained in the face of the obvious difficulties of fox hunting in the mountains. Even with the best of luck it is seldom that a fox hunt gives an opportunity for a gallop in this broken country, and to get variety and better sport Rachel turned to the idea of drags. In this, as with her first hounds, she was helped by Jack Boyd and endeavored to model her drags on those he had developed in Southern Pines. Local landowners showed the heartiest cooperation and the country was pretty well paneled, so well, in fact, that there were no strict, conventional drag lines and a drag could be laid almost anywhere, much as a fox might run. The line was laid without the master or whips knowing, except generally, how it might run, and in this way natural hunting conditions were duplicated. The best of these drags were in the Jackson River bottoms, although there was most attractive country in the southern end of the Valley near Falling Springs. There were also drags in the Valley near Hot Springs but the amount of forest cover and the nature of the terrain there did not give the same scope to producing natural hunting conditions as did the other localities.

At its peak the Bath County Hounds met three times a week, twice for drags and once for live fox. Some of the fox hunts were classics; seldom was it possible to kill, but the hounds were often out from dawn to dusk. One wise old fox, usually jumped near Bacova, inevitably denned in safety in the rocks on top of Little Mountain over

Germantown. How the few left in the field, including my wife, ever got to the finish on thoroughbreds is still a marvel to me. Another fox jumped often on the Queen Farm and finally reached safety in the cliffs along Cowardin's Run below Groce's Spring.

Often horses and hounds were loaded into a van to go farther afield. Besides the meet at Ed Porter's on the Cowpasture, there was a famous one at the Shiflett Farm on the road to Deerfield. The fields, naturally, were never large; I think the top was forty, at a drag when a number of people came over from Staunton. Usually the field was from eight to twenty.

Our family acquired a number of hunters and our four children, when home, came out. Until away at school and college two of them, Abbie and Susie, acted as whips. Many of the local country folk came out. I shall never forget Jimmie Mines, the husband of "Miss Sally" at Fassifern. Jimmie must have weighed around two hundred and fifty pounds and rode "By Grace and By God." An animated meal sack, he bounced about on a rough but capable horse and always came through, although some of the going on the drags was by no means easy, with many of the jumps well over four feet. Rachel had high class horses and believed in making her drags real hunts, with the line laid by a man who knew the way of foxes, and the jumps such as would be met in any hunting field. The excitement of hunting is contagious and an amusing example of this occurred on one drag. One of the local residents asked if she might bring a guest and said she hoped the jumps would not be over three feet six inches that day as the guest was an elderly man and there might be an accident. Rachel was a bit miffed and said he would have to take things as they came. The hounds got off the line at one point and the field found itself behind a rather stiff in and out jump. Rachel, riding her magnificent big three-quarter bred gray, went at the jump and over but the rest milled around, with refusals and general confusion. Out of the melee came the old gentleman straight and true for the fence and, with a whoop, led the rest over.

Dr. Ruddle, the local veterinarian, was almost always along. One famous jump became known as his. He had the most miraculous ability of coming down from great heights to land again in the saddle and after a few bobbles be going again. His jump was from a field into the highway and a gallery was usually present to watch him take it. I never heard of his failing to hit that saddle but often wondered how he did it. Incidentally he rode a horse called Black Dick. Dick had run in the Maryland Gold Cup but fell on evil days after sundry changes of masters, finally being traded off by a horse dealer for a hound.

Once in a while someone staying at the hotel would be asked to join, and the Homestead stables had a few horses capable of going well, but hotel visitors were never much of a factor. The nucleus of every meet was our family and those for whom Rachel provided mounts, with some few farmers and other local residents.

A few years ago the formal Bath County Hounds were disbanded. Trouble began to be experienced with deer, which became so plentiful as to make much of the country unusable. There was one gallop across the Dinwiddie Meadows, the whips trying to whip off the hounds from a herd of six deer, which ultimately jumped the wire fence by the river bank, swam the stream and left for parts unknown, carrying with them a sizable number of hounds. Then some of the local supporters for one reason and another dropped out, satisfactory whips were not to be had, and the crowning blow was the meat shortage during the war with hounds to feed. Today we have in the kennel just one hound, old Julep, the third generation of that name. The others were dispersed one way or another. The probabilities are that if you hear the hounds on a moonlight night, some will be descendants of those so long kenneled at The Yard.

The raising of horses still goes on. We almost had a farm on Long Island, but labor and other things were pretty high there and when we had finished building a house and garage there was not much left for stables, etc. Now at Hot Springs, where pasture is easier to find and farm labor available, almost as soon as we were established we began to look for a real farm.

On the face of things the best farming land in mountain country is along the river valleys and we looked at many of these. We could not find anything which did not have some objectionable features and were getting discouraged when an unexpected opportunity arose. The Company was acquiring all the springs possible for water supply and in buying these tried to get enough surrounding land to protect them from contamination. Whole farms had to be bought at times as the owners would not sell the water rights, to be left with land and no water. Mostly these springs are on the side of the Warm Springs Mountain at about 3,000 feet elevation, where the limestone basic deposits join the overlying sandstone. Two such farms were bought in 1925, one from Elisha Karnes and another from William M. McAllister. When Rachel saw these she fell in love with them. Although dotted with rock outcrops and having many steep slopes, the bluegrass grows luxuriantly. There is one field on the McAllister place in bluegrass sod which for over a hundred years has never been broken by a plow. This high country bluegrass in limestone territory has great nutritive value, how much can be seen by the fact that a few years later when she did not have sufficient stock for the grass that was growing, Rachel was able to get for pasturing fattening steers just twice what the farmers in rich Eastern Virginia or along the river bottoms could obtain. The Company bought these two farms and then I bought from it, ex-water except for a small supply, the Mc-Allister place. The Karnes farm was put into immediate use by the Company, to provide pasture for the livery horses and a place where good sound mares, too old for livery use, could be bred and their colts raised, to take their place ultimately in the stable.

For a time we had nothing but horses on Hobby Horse Farm, as it was named, but while there are quite a few there still, including two stallions and a few brood mares with their babies, the main emphasis is now on the placid, regal Shorthorn beef animal.

Hobby Horse Farm has become one of the great personal joys of my life. Its location is truly magnificent, on a huge shoulder or spur jutting off from the main mass of Warm Springs Mountain at an elevation of just about three thousand feet. Rising abruptly behind it to the east is the steep slope going up to Bald Knob, while off to the west one can see range after range of mountains, with High Point on Alleghany Mountain, in West Virginia, in the distance.

We built a log cabin and the work was done by men who had lived in such themselves and had helped build many. It was built as the old-time cabins were, with the latches for the doors wooden contraptions whittled out by hand. There is one Yale lock but all others are what the mountaineers used, and "the latch string out" has a real meaning at Hobby Horse. Two miles from the main floor of the Valley and with intervening ridges, you can watch the sun go down behind the hills. No noise of auto horn can be heard and the silence is only broken by the lowing of a cow or the baying of a dog running on the hills above. Once a year Rachel insists that servants come to clean but for the balance of the time the somewhat incongruous, completely modern kitchen is presided over by the writer while Rachel does the housework. It is the sort of retreat where, like Antaeus, you can get renewed vigor by near contact with the soil.

## 23. *Reorganization*

IN BUILDING the million-dollar tower, an inevitable
error was made. It was not foreseen what was going
to happen in 1929 and the tower was not adequately
financed. Together with a good many millions of other
Americans, we did not anticipate the lean years ahead,
and the ownership of the Hot Springs Company became,
in consequence, a liability instead of an asset. This
lack of foresight was to bring The Homestead, the Company, and in fact the whole Valley to the brink of ruin.
For me, personally, it was going to mean ten years of the

hardest work I ever performed and an education in a lot of things about which I knew nothing.

The crash of 1929 knocked the bottom out of The Homestead's business. A huge proportion of its clientele died, either physically or financially. Among others to suffer were the members of the New York Stock Exchange who had been coming here, many of whom never recovered.

When 1930 came around and it was obvious that business was going to be inadequate, we all expected that the collapse would only be temporary. Something of the same sort had happened in 1907 and again in 1921, but this time there was no come-back.

In December of 1931 I went for a short duck shooting trip on the Potomac, going by car and returning on the twentieth. As I topped the Warm Springs Mountain I saw the car which was used by Andersen, our manager, and as I drove up young Bobby Andersen flagged me down; I leaned out of the car window to have him tell me brokenly that his father had dropped dead the day before.

I had been president of the Company since 1922 but during that time knew in only a general way what really went on in the operation of the hotel. There had been plenty of other matters to keep me busy, with the multifarious activities of the Company, and, having early satisfied myself as to Andersen's ability and integrity, for the hotel itself left everything in his hands. Andersen had no understudy, and our principal activity was without a head. Naturally, my first thought was that we must have another manager. I called a directors' meeting and had a candidate for consideration. By that time the mistakes made in financing the tower were beginning to pinch. Income was less than outgo and my brothers and I had begun to put up money to keep in operation. Now I know we should have pulled the plug at once when the figures began to run red. In the long run it would have cost us less and a reorganization then would have been no more painful than it was when it finally came in 1938. However, that was the situation when we had our meeting. I presented the facts and named my candidate. Andersen had been getting $20,000 a year and my brother, George, asked where we were going to get the money for the new manager and everything else. Then, remarking that I had been at Hot Springs for nine years and seemed to be in good health, he asked why I could not carry on without a manager. The proposal almost took my breath away, and if I had known then as much about running a hotel as I do now I would have said it was impossible. However, to use Wetmore's words, "I was not afraid of the cars" and said if I could think of some man in the organization whom I could use to keep me from making silly technical mistakes I would try the job.

There were several young men in our employ whom I thought had ability but I finally made what proved a wise choice, in selecting George Slosson, Jr. Slosson was young but had worked in hotels all his business life, much of the time at The Homestead though with intermissions, and at that particular time was purchasing agent. I could count on Slosson's honesty and industry and soon found he had excellent powers of organization. We plunged into the job and made an efficient working team for the next decade. I first made him assistant to the president, then manager, and finally general manager.

I was determined to know thoroughly what went on back stage, and immediately discovered a sad situation.

The attack which took Andersen off had not come without warning, as heart trouble had crippled him for the previous four years. While it did not affect his mind, it slowed him physically so that he could not get around, and to do the job well a manager of a hotel has to be over his plant unceasingly. Laxity had crept in, both in maintenance and in the working organization. There was an immense amount to be done and, to add to our difficulties, no money to do it with. We had to make our bricks without straw.

It was not only in the technical operation of the hotel that things had slipped but, perhaps more, in our guest relations. There was no doubt a certain amount of complacency in the twenties so that no one realized that the clientele of a hotel is never static but must be continually renewed. Not much attention had been paid to getting new and younger visitors and when the cataclysm of '29 wiped out so many of the old, little was left. For this part of the job I eventually got Clarence Madden, a curious individual. He should have been a scholar and author but all he ever wrote was a book on Advertising Hotels, really an authority on the subject, and a number of short articles on cats. Now a cat is about the only member of the animal kingdom which strikes no sympathetic chord with me, and that made it hard going at first. I found later that Madden had a fine appreciation of all literature and became fond of him. He made me do a lot of things I'd said I would never do and generally gave me an education in public relations which was invaluable.

Some of my attempts at being a hotel manager were neither orthodox nor conventional. One of the first tasks facing us was employing a new chef. Slosson got in touch with Francois Dulom, who was ultimately engaged and is still with us. Dulom was then working in Dayton,

Ohio, and could not come to The Homestead for an interview, but the mountain was movable so Slosson and I arranged to meet him in Cincinnati. I was perfectly aware that I knew nothing about a hotel kitchen but I also knew, from his record, that Dulom was entirely competent. If I knew little about the work the chef was going to be called upon to perform, I believed I was a pretty good judge of character and personality. However capable for the particular job, I wanted to be sure of two things, first, that any man who came to The Homestead was going to find an environment in which he would be happy and, second, that he had the sort of personality that would make it easy for me and others to work with him.

There was no use considering a man who did not like country life, so I began to probe Dulom on that point. I found we had a mutual love for fishing. He and I at once began to talk fishing at Hot Springs—not a word was said about the job at The Homestead. We had a limited time at our disposal and I could see Slosson getting more and more nervous. He kept edging to the front of his chair until he was almost sitting on air. At last he could stand it no longer and interrupted the fishing talk to say we had to catch our train and that nothing had been decided. When he was through, I said to Dulom, "I am satisfied if you are." Then I told him the salary. He thought for a few minutes and then said, "I will take the job." It may be said that I hired a chef because he liked to fish but of course I knew before the interview that he could cook. Furthermore, I have never had reason to change the opinion I then formed of his character while discussing something entirely foreign to the job for which he was employed. Therewith commenced an association of sixteen years, still going strong, which has certainly been a source of satisfaction and pleasure to me and I hope to Dulom as well.

I made it a point to question everything and found many things being done only because they had always been done. There is a story which has served me in good stead. We were having the butcher shop repainted and one of the old workmen with whom I had played as a boy was painting a motor. I saw him working at it for two days, while I knew he had finished three others the first day. "Why does it take so long to paint that motor, Frank?" I asked. "You painted three in less time." "Well," he replied, "you see this is a red motor." I asked why it was red and the only explanation was that it always had been. After that when I did not think some process made sense I used to ask if the thing was another red motor. The whole organization came right up on its toes to the question, until a "red motor" became a by-word.

Money was raised by all sorts of means, mostly by members of the Ingalls family digging down and putting up. Business slowly began to come back, when we came to the end of our string financially. For the building of the tower only about $300,000 of actual new money was raised. The balance was provided out of surplus funds and by increasing the floating debt. The Ingalls family bought preferred stock, then a second mortgage. Then a loan was obtained by the Company from the Federal Reserve Bank. We had forgotten all about the bonds, a million of them, issued in 1891 and due in 1941, but it now became obvious that with the maturity of the bank loan and that of the 1891 mortgage so close, and an abnormally large floating indebtedness, some sort of bankruptcy proceeding was inevitable.

We applied for a receivership before the State Courts and I was appointed receiver. The Chesapeake and Ohio Railway held $385,000 of the 1891 bonds and almost immediately forced a transfer of the legal action into the Federal Courts with a proceeding under Chapter X of the new Chandler Act (old Section 77-B of the Bankruptcy Act). Otto Miller, at the request of the Railway, was made Trustee in Bankruptcy and I was continued as Executive Manager. Under this Bankruptcy Act the holders of twenty-five per cent of any class of securities can veto any plan of reorganization. The Railway held forty per cent of the 1891 bond issue, and Molotov could have learned from them the use of the veto. It would have been wiser if the Ingalls family, holding approximately the same amount of these bonds and a majority of the other obligations of the Company, had insisted on a foreclosure and sale, but George Ingalls had died, Albert was ill, and I did not feel I could take such responsibility for the family. In the end a reorganization was worked out, practically dictated by the Railway as they promptly vetoed any plan not entirely to their liking. What made the situation particularly galling to me was that the Railway had an immense investment in The Greenbrier, at White Sulphur, our nearest if not our chief competitor.

Generally speaking, the real powers in the Railway were disposed to be fair, but, probably because of their familiarity with the traditionally heavy operating losses at The Greenbrier, they could not see how we could ever expect to make money at The Homestead. To no avail we pointed out The Homestead's record of successful operation from 1891 until caught by the unfortunate coincidence of construction of the tower and maturity of a million dollar bond issue while the nation was still suffering from its worst economic crisis. Naturally, we could not with delicacy suggest that losses at White Sulphur and profits at Hot Springs might possibly be the difference between railroad and private management. Being so confident that we could not make a go of it, these gentlemen would have nothing less than a mortgage on all of our property (in which they would have a one-third share) securing their financial interest, with a provision in this mortgage that they should have the right to name two directors for the new Company. They wanted to be in a position, as they expressed it, "to buy the property at foreclosure without putting up any more money, and thus assure the continued operation of a valuable source of railroad traffic." Had it not been that Earle Bailie, a visitor at The Homestead for many years and a personal friend of the writer, became a dominant figure in the railroad just at the crucial point of the reorganization, even what was saved would have been lost. Unfortunately, he died before the reorganization could be completed, but it had progressed so far by that time that the plan was carried through.

We had one piece of luck. The Company, up to the time of the crisis, never had a general counsel nor had I personally had occasion to need the services of a Virginia lawyer. Now it became imperative that we have legal guidance and that it be of the best. I had known of Frank W. Rogers, of Roanoke, by reputation and casual acquaintanceship and employed him. The combination of a fine legal mind and excellent business judgment which he brought to us did as much as any one factor to save the situation.

Rogers fought hard to secure a plan which would eliminate bonds with securing mortgages and substitute stock for the various interests, which would have made possible a sound and workable corporate structure. He was unable to accomplish this but did succeed in getting for the old equity interests stock in the new company—stock which then seemed to have only the most remote gambler's possibility of value.

In the end, on March 31, 1940, the properties were turned back to the real owners, with the Railway Company retaining the right to name two directors. The financial structure of the new company was so cumbersome and inadequate that it did not seem as if it could last for even a few years, but the tide of business had already begun to turn and in seven years it was possible to again achieve a strong position, with no one who had stuck by the Company losing anything.

Today the only interest which the Cheasapeake and Ohio Railway has in The Homestead or Hot Springs is the same it has in the prosperity of any large source of revenue from freight and passenger traffic along its lines.

When the reorganization was completed the work of rehabilitation went right along. Even while in the hands of the courts all surplus income was devoted to that purpose. However, in spite of return of business, funds were short and when there came a chance to sell a subsidiary, the Valley Electric Company, it was taken advantage of and the money realized went back into The Homestead, practically rebuilding the main section.

The story of the Valley Electric is much like that of all development here. Although the Valley had been settled for many years and had a considerable population, about four thousand in the area directly dominated by the Company, as far as the march of the industrial age is concerned it was completely isolated. This did not materially change with the growth of The Homestead Hotel and outside its doors, except where it exerted a direct influence, things remained about as they were. The type of settlement in the Valley was semi-rural, that is made up of scattered dwellings, with no town, only in a few places a small number of houses closer together than the average, usually gathered around the nucleus of an old-fashioned country store. There were no incorporated towns, no public water supply or sewerage system, no power lines, no telephones, not even police protection except that afforded by the sheriff. All of these services gradually came to be supplied by the Company, first for the necessities of The Homestead Hotel, then for its employees who must live near by, and, in the end, for the benefit of the community generally. The result was that this became pretty nearly a self-sufficient community, with the Company directing a "managed economy."

Back in 1891 when the Virginia Hotel was built, a power plant was put in to provide electric light and heat. Gradually the power lines were extended to one house after another, first to the stores and few dwellings immediately adjacent to the powerhouse. As soon as one house got current, the next-door neighbor would plead for just a few yards further extension, and it was hard to find a reason why it could not be had. The camel got his head under the tent when the first connection was made, and he wriggled constantly and actively in. Gradually power lines were extended until finally the Valley from Warm Springs to Healing Springs was covered with a network of distribution lines. Franchises were obtained and the Valley Electric Company was formed. Additional steam and electric generating equipment was put in the hotel's powerhouse and a sizable and profitable electric utility established.

Then a curious fact developed, quite characteristic of the unconventional way in which all growth has taken place in the Valley. So long as the hotel could use the exhaust steam from the powerhouse, electricity could be generated cheaply from reciprocating engines and all was lovely. However, people would keep using more electricity and it came to a point where steam was going off into the atmosphere and the cost of current skyrocketed. I came to dread each month's statement showing greater sales, an anomalous position for the head of a utility. The State Commission would not permit of discouraging consumption by raising rates, even if I could have lived in the community had I been responsible for so doing. Service had to be excellent, for the same lines that served the community generally also supplied the Cascades Inn and Club, dairy and other outlying parts of the Company property.

There were two alternatives, one to spend a lot of money installing modern generating equipment, or to get current from some larger power company. We had no money and the only large power company anywhere near was a utility in financial difficulties. The situation was getting serious when Uncle Sam came along with his Rural Electrification Agency. After long and complicated negotiations the Valley Electric was sold to this Agency at a bargain price, and the cash just at that time was a godsend.

This sale was to a cooperative and the natural assumption was that public opinion would be all for government ownership. It didn't work out that way and for quite a while it looked as if the deal would fall through for want of support by those who would be the customers. After the sale the cooperative had its troubles, and only recently have people ceased coming to me to express regret that the transfer was made. From all this I got complete confirmation of what I always suspected, that financially, whatever may be said sociologically, government operation of power companies is inefficient and shot through with misrepresentation and "buncombe."

Much the same situation arose with the telephone service but this came later when money was more plentiful and expansion did not require such an outlay, so the Company is still in the telephone business. Even at that, a sale was contemplated and thereby hangs a tale which always amuses me, typifying as it does the engineer's point of view.

Negotiations were almost completed and it was apparent that we would just about break even financially on the sale. Good service is of the utmost importance to the hotel, and I investigated that. It was a toss-up if local and hotel service would be improved, but I was assured that long distance would be immensely better. "We would improve that a hundred per cent" was the statement. I pricked up my ears and asked what that meant. The reply was that the time to make a station-to-station call from Hot Springs to New York would be cut from ninety seconds to forty-five, just one hundred per cent. I admitted the percentage was all right although phrased backward, but could not see that for guests at The Homestead saving forty-five seconds on a call to New York was going to be a material factor in their happiness and comfort while here, not nearly as important as being sure the girls who handled the call were under discipline and training by the hotel and not by some far-off superintendent; a courteous reply to a room service order would mean more than forty-five seconds wait, and the sale never went through.

## 24. The Japanese Invasion

WHEN NEWS of the bombing of Pearl Harbor broke on the world there was immediately speculation as to how war would affect The Homestead. The only guide to thinking was the experience during the first World War. At that time the effect on The Homestead was really insignificant, a drop in business on declaration of war and then a gradual return until at the end of the first year more people were coming than ever before.

Naturally, the first war did not leave The Homestead completely untouched. It ruined the career of the manager who was here at that time. There were also the typical spy scares. Mrs. Carlisle, who was living in her house on the hill in front of The Homestead, had an electric light in the attic, hanging by a cord, and, from drafts or otherwise, this would swing from side to side. As it swung, its rays were interrupted by the mullions in the attic window. Some of the old ladies (I am not sure of which sex) who sat on the front porch of evenings noticed this and became convinced there was signaling of important war secrets going on. To whom such secrets could be transmitted by such a means, why this complicated Oppenheim method was adopted, or what secrets were to be learned at Hot Springs did not present difficulties to these patriots. One of the reasons for the German manager's lack of popularity was that he refused to take the matter seriously. Not so the observers, among whom was one of sufficient prominence so that her letter to Washington brought the Secret Service to Hot Springs to investigate. I would like to see the report they turned in.

For a short time after America's entry into World War II life moved along uneventfully. Then one day I received a telephone call from a Chesapeake and Ohio representative in Washington asking if The Homestead was prepared to make its facilities available for a war purpose involving the housing of five hundred persons who were going to be interned. The idea did not appeal but it was shortly explained that while this was a request from the State Department it was a wartime "request or else." Under the circumstances there was nothing to do but agree gracefully. I was advised a representative of the State Department would arrive shortly to tell us the bad news and make final arrangements.

A few days later a charming, able and straightforward gentleman, Stanley Woodward, arrived from the State Department and we went into a huddle. The people we were to house were the Japanese internees, made up of the diplomatic and consular forces, representatives of the Japanese press, and some prominent businessmen. We were told that the treatment accorded these Japs would determine how our people in similar straits in Japan would fare and our responsibility to help our own unfortunates was stressed. We were told that the F. B. I. would deliver the Japs to Hot Springs and that a detachment of the Border Patrol would guard them. No one was to be allowed in The Homestead except the staff of the hotel and the official party. The Japanese were to receive the same service and the same quality of food which was standard for other Homestead guests. Promises were made that there would be at least 400, and a hard bargain was driven by the State Department on the basis that with assurance of uniform number and no turnover it would be a cheap operation, particularly as the State Department guaranteed payment for damage from vandalism. All guests were to be vacated from The Homestead by December fifteenth, 1941.

In the end The Homestead lost a small fortune. The first Jap did not arrive until December twenty-ninth and, although the organization had been built up to take care of 400, the number did not reach 300 until the twentieth of February and the top at any time was 363. The rate fixed barely allowed The Homestead to break even when the full complement was on hand and, of course, left no margin to make up for the time when only a handful were here or to compensate for the

elimination of the spring season. However, it probably
saved the hotel from a worse fate, use as a barracks or
the like.

The stay of the Jap contingent was both humorous
and tragic. It was intensely irritating to the staff of the
hotel from the beginning, when they were subjected to
screening by the F. B. I., going into all sorts of details of
their personal lives, until they finished putting the hotel
back in order after the evacuation. It is a matter for
great satisfaction that out of almost a thousand employees
the F. B. I. never found anything against one, and that, in
spite of great provocation at times, I never heard of a
single instance of discourtesy or failure to give service to
the Japs.

Unending questions have been asked and are still
coming about how the Japs behaved while at The Homestead. With a guard for almost every three Japs and
F. B. I. men on duty twenty-four hours a day, they did
not have much opportunity to do anything except what
they were told. Nearly all came from the better classes
and their education comprised, in particular, obedience
to higher authority, and they had their official superiors
here with them. Most of the few unpleasant incidents
came when they wanted to show their jubilation over the
fall of Singapore or some similar success. After all,
though unreasonable, it was impossible not to be irritated
on walking by their bulletin board covered with characters, to hear the cackling and hissing expressions of
pleasure at what they read there. In the very few cases
of actual discourtesy, apology was promptly made by
the Ambassador.

Many of the Jap social customs seemed strange, such
as the precedence of men over women entering an elevator,
or women, already seated at the table, rising if a man came

later. It was hard, too, to become accustomed to the drab dresses of the women. However one learned to accept these things, and association with some of the English-speaking internees produced a real liking. Many of those people had lived their whole lives in America and a few were as genuinely loyal to the United States and its institutions as an alien of any race could be.

There were, of course, incidents of a kind of wiliness which we have become accustomed to associate with the Japanese character. One of these had an amusing denouement. On being interned the Japs were allowed to keep their papers and these were held inviolate. They could not quite believe this was true. They were not the only ones who felt that such a policy was quixotic and more and more, as time went on, many of us felt aggrieved that protocol prevented our learning what might be in records so completely within our control. One Jap became so worried that he determined to destroy his documents and for that purpose kindled a nice little fire in his bathtub. He didn't realize the delicacy of the sprinkler system, which promptly went off. Guards, F. B. I. and hotel staff rushed to the room where the indicator showed a fire. There never was a more bedraggled and pitiful figure than that found on breaking in, a poor, skinny little man, standing in the bathtub, dressed in a pair of shorts, slinky long black hair plastered over his face, desperately trying to nurse the fire and ward off the downpour.

It must be remembered that The Homestead was so thoroughly guarded that it was almost as difficult to get in as it would be to get out of Sing Sing Prison. There was a cordon of sentry boxes, floodlights all about, and at every possible entrance trigger-happy guards demanding "Who goes there?" One evening a group was sitting in front of the fire near the clock in the main lobby. About all the notables were there. There were the F. B. I. men not on duty, the Commander of the Border Patrol, Poole, a delightful gentleman representing the State Department, the Spanish Attache, supposed to see that no Jap was given the third degree, and quite a few Japs. One of the latter, a press photographer, was telling us of the telegram he got from the A. P. when he sent some unsatisfactory pictures of the tour of an American professional ball team in Japan, reading "Buy yourself for fifty cents a Spalding guide and get pictures that look like baseball." He got even with them later when the Japs invaded China and he got a request for pictures of the bombing of a Chinese city. He replied, "Spend fifty cents for a Rand-McNally atlas and remember my country is at war with China and your city one thousand miles within a hostile country."

All was peaceful and quiet when an immaculately groomed military police rushed up out of breath. Saluting the Commander of the Border Patrol, he announced, "Sir, there is a strange Japanese girl trying to get into The Homestead." The conference broke up as if a bomb had burst. In a few minutes, accompanied by the authorities, a Japanese girl, looking as amused as a Jap can, was ushered in between two hulking M. P.s. It seems this girl was one of the staff of the Japanese Consulate in San Francisco. The rest of her associates were picked up by the F. B. I. and transported to Hot Springs but no one had said anything to her. She began to get lonesome walking around the San Francisco streets and to be annoyed, as any Jap would, so she decided she ought to join the others at Hot Springs. Without any difficulty, she bought a ticket to Chicago. There she tried to buy a ticket to Hot Springs but that destination was marked off the railway schedules. She studied the maps and bought one for Cincinnati, taking the night train, after spending the afternoon in the Shedd Aquarium. In Cincinnati she again could not get a ticket to Hot Springs but got one to Covington, Virginia. She spent the morning shopping and took the noon train. Arriving in Covington she had real trouble. By that time she was near the firing line and no taxi driver would take her. In the end she got a brave man to drive her up, letting her out in sight of The Homestead. He did not want to get mixed up with a Jap, so collected his fare, got her out of the cab and beat it as fast as he could, leaving her to talk with the guard.

After everything was over an account was written of the occupation and printed in a small pamphlet. Reluctantly, permission was given to distribute this among a few people, such as the directors of the Company, but it had to be marked confidential. As originally written the pamphlet may have been a bit spicy but before even the limited publication was allowed it had to pass the censor for the State Department, the F. B. I. and the Border Patrol. I never could see that it disclosed any military secrets but it perhaps stepped on the toes of the organizations which did the censoring and when they were all through it was somewhat emasculated.

The above story of the gal from San Francisco, which I liked particularly, was deleted with others because, obviously, it indicated that someone had blundered, but I see no reason why it cannot be told now. The State Department was supposed to give to the F. B. I. the names of the Jap Consular forces and the F. B. I. to catch them. That made it look as if the joke was on the State Department, but that department countered by saying that the F. B. I., even if names were not given, ought not to have left a Japanese official running around loose. It was impossible to fix definite responsibility and everyone's feelings might be hurt so the compromise was reached that the whole story should be hush hush and no one would be blamed.

Getting rid of the Japs had its dramatic moments. The high light came when I went to a prominent member of Congress and asked him to put pressure on the State Department to move them elsewhere. We had a good case, as there had been verbal assurance that the hotel would be released to us by spring, and we had alternative places of residence to suggest, but things moved slowly. While I was in my friend's office he called the State Department and got an Assistant Secretary on the phone. Of course I only heard one end of the conversation but watched the Congressman getting more and more testy as the talk went on, and then heard his final shot. "I don't give a damn what you do about Heaven and Earth. What I want is for you to move those Japs." It is easy enough to guess what the bedeviled Secretary had said.

When the time finally came for the Japs to leave, the famous telegram to Homestead guests was sent, reading—"The Japs are gone and Spring is here." In spite of this The Homestead opened on Easter Sunday with only twenty-two guests.

I cannot leave the story of the Japanese at Hot Springs without an apology to a man I had thought and said was a snake in the grass of the lowest order.

When the great day came at last for the Japs to leave in April, 1942, a special train was provided. I was at the station to see them off and received word that Ambassador Nomura wished to say good-bye to me. He was in a private car at the rear of the train and I climbed on board and found him sitting in the observa-

tion end. He held out his hand to me, and said a few
formal and conventional words, thanking me for the
way in which his people had been treated, then continued:
"This is a most unfortunate situation, Mr. Ingalls, and
entirely unnecessary. I hope some day to come back to
your beautiful mountains and play golf with you. Our
people should be friends and this war never would have
come about except for a few wilful and ambitious men."
This was at the time when the Japanese were trying to
put the blame for the war on Roosevelt. I was no admirer of Roosevelt but am an American and reserve to
my fellow citizens the right to criticize our President,
and this, coming from a Jap, stiffened every sinew and
cartilage in my backbone. I did my best to imitate a
frozen-faced Englishman and, with a stiff bow from the
hips, said "Good-bye, Mr. Ambassador" and backed out
of the train with blood pressure high enough to break a
sphygmomanometer.

While the Japanese were at Hot Springs I had many
talks with Roy Morgan, in charge of the F. B. I. personnel, about Nomura and Kurusu and whether or not
they were both "double-crossing" this country or perhaps each other. Morgan insisted that the verdict for
Nomura must be "not proven" but I was sceptical and
this interview seemed to clinch my opinion.

I saw Roy Morgan again in 1947. Since his tour of
duty at Hot Springs he had left the F. B. I. and become
a successful attorney in Greensboro, North Carolina,
but in the interim he had been in Japan, assisting in the
prosecution of war criminals. Morgan told me he had had
access to the most secret Japanese archives and among
these had found three telegrams from Nomura to the
home office, sent during the summer and fall before the
attack on Pearl Harbor. I recall the substance though

not the exact wording of these dispatches, as told to me by Morgan. Each was a request to be allowed to resign his post and return to Japan. As a reason, he said he had had a long career in the diplomatic service, during which he had served faithfully and to the best of his ability. He said he had never done a dishonorable thing in the whole of his career but now, stationed in a country for which he had a great friendship, he felt that in carrying out his instructions he was being compelled to act dishonestly. There followed the usual protestations of loyalty to the Emperor and the request that he be allowed to retire before he would have to sully a long career full of honors.

These dispatches were at first ignored, and then he was curtly informed he must continue to follow instructions. Morgan also told me that Nomura was cooperative and helpful in unscrambling the whole cabal of the war party in Japan. I feel now that Nomura was trying to tell me, so far as he could without open disloyalty to his government, that he thought its policies were wrong. He could not have gone farther any more than could I have listened to a criticism of our President. My lack of perspicacity made me and not Nomura act the cad in this last interview, and I am glad now to make a public apology to a man who I believe, in the light of later knowledge, was an honorable gentleman and true patriot.

# 25. The Food Conference

THE JAPS left and life began to return to normal
at The Homestead. However there were rumblings
and uncertainties. The Greenbrier was taken by the
Army for a hospital and every branch of the government
was looking for housing for one purpose or another,
ranging from a school for WACs to hospitals. Long
negotiations were held with the Surgeon General regarding
the use of The Homestead as some sort of Army hospital.
It became obvious from these that if any government

department commandeered The Homestead it would mean financial ruin. There could be no compensation for one hundred years of tradition, and in calculating the value the desperately poverty-stricken years during the depression would be used as a yardstick. I have often wondered at the stories of immense sums paid for properties seized by the government and, after my experiences, am amazed that such things should happen. Certainly the men I dealt with were as close traders and as careful of Uncle Sam's pocketbook as would have been any private buyer. In fact, they were harder to deal with, for at all times I was conscious they held the whip hand. They were sympathetic with our problems but in much the same way that a commander is when, for the general good, he sends his men into conflict with the probability of death.

The Army for all sorts of reasons did not like the idea of The Homestead for a hospital. It was not entirely a steel and concrete structure, it was on a branch line of the railroad, and the physical layout was wrong for a hospital, even worse than The Greenbrier, with which they were already becoming dissatisfied. Besides, negotiations were going to be most complicated because of our telephone operations for the local community, golf links, water systems and a host of other activities for which they would have to pay something, even if not much. I was beginning to feel more comfortable, believing the Army would leave us alone, when one day I heard the Navy had decided to take The Homestead. There had been no preliminary discussion with any of the Navy medical staff, but the latter apparently had access to the Army reports and felt satisfied. It looked like the end of the rope, when there came a bolt from the blue in the form of a telephone call from the State Department advising that they wanted The Homestead for a most important international conference which was to be held in this country. I blessed my soul that we had done the good job we did with the Japs and had managed to get over all the rough spots with the Department, and there were a few, when the Japs were here. I knew it was going to mean the loss of a lot of money, but the conference could not be interminable as would be a hospital and, furthermore, it would not be necessary to break up our organization. So I jumped at the opportunity but told my friends in the State Department that it might be too late as I understood the Navy had already drawn and signed the papers to commandeer the place. There was a bit of a pause when I gave this information—apparently someone held the wire while my statement was repeated— then I was told to go right ahead with our preparations and if necessary the Department would go next door, on Pennsylvania Avenue, to put the Navy in its place. Apparently this was done, for I got a most ill-natured phone call from the Navy, in which I was told to mind my own business and that representatives of the Navy would be on hand in a few days to settle all details. I did not know where we stood but no one showed up from the Navy, and in a few days we were deep in arrangements to handle the first of the international conferences, that on world food problems.

Arrangements for the conference were made in great detail by the State Department, as they were for the Japs. I was impressed by the minuteness with which things were worked out and by the efficiency of the Department. If, in the end, the affair gave me a contempt for international conferences of any sort, at least I had to admit that, so far as staging a show of this sort was concerned, the staff of the Department knew its business.

The Conference was held from May seventeenth to June fourth, 1943, with all the pomp which a meeting of allied nations should command. The thing which made it seem almost ridiculous was the way in which the Press was handled. Apparently Roosevelt was afraid of the Press and the most elaborate precautions were taken to see that all reporters were kept from coming in contact with the delegates except under the watchful eye of Marvin Jones, Chairman of the Conference. The delegates were housed in The Homestead but the Press got rooms where they could in the neighborhood and were allotted the casino in which to work. Once a day, en masse, they were allowed to come into The Homestead, but never individually. Obviously enough, representatives of sovereign powers could not be kept within bounds as were the Japs, and many of their own initiative saw the reporters. While no representative of the Press might go within The Homestead except for formal communiques, nothing could stop the delegates from going to the casino. The result was a good deal of hard feeling but no secrecy.

There was much grandiloquence and apparently as much woozy thinking as could be found in any high school auditorium. I heard a lot of the talk, both informal and for publication, and, though there undoubtedly were present many able and high-principled men, it struck me that most were just trying to get some of the pickings Uncle Sam was supposed to be ready to throw around. I got fed up with the sham and hypocrisy and one night sat down to write what I called "A Worm's-Eye View of the First International Food Conference." I picked this up a few days ago and while it may seem a bit crude and unfair, as a backstairs report written contemporaneously

it has some interest. Having seen what subsequent conferences did or did not accomplish, I have less reluctance
in giving my impressions of this one. Here is the story . . .

\* \* \* \* \* \*

## THE EMBATTLED TRENCHERMEN

There is all the setting for a classic Gilbert and
Sullivan operetta at The Homestead. If only the two
hundred stenographers, translators, mimeograph operators and filing clerks of the State Department of the
United States and forty-two other nations had been
picked with greater regard for pulchritude, it would be
perfect. However, chorus girls and boys never look as
well out of costume and I shall not be surprised if they
make a better showing when they come dancing down the
lobby in gay and abbreviated raiment.

We are perfectly equipped for the soldiers' chorus.
The detachment of military police, a picked body of men,
trained to the last minute, have an excellent band with
a glorious bass drummer. Wearing spic and span uniforms
trimmed with white, they are ubiquitous, stationed at
every door and entrance. At 6:45 (apologies, at 18:45)
they mount the guard and strike the colors. The show
at Buckingham Palace does not surpass that put on in
front of The Homestead, with the band playing and
snappy drill and inspection. As all stand at attention
while the bugle blows and the colors are slowly lowered,
it is most effective. There are two hundred soldiers and
to see that they are well commanded there are a colonel,
two majors, three captains, and a few lieutenants thrown
in for good measure.

We have a band of outlaws skulking in the offing,
endeavoring to seduce the Trenchermen but kept at a
safe distance by the military. There are some fifty of

these guerrillas of the press, each seeking how more effectively he can stick his knife into the staff. They have all the properties which a million-dollar movie production would call for. The casino is set up with long tables lined with typewriters, and behind them all sorts of transmitting equipment, from the oldest sort of Morse telegraph keys through the gamut, including teletype machines, tickers and apparatus for transmitting photographs by wire. Nestling among the typewriters are plenty of half full glasses and completely inadequate bushel basket ash receivers. The outlaws gather in chain smoking groups and seem to be continuously engaged in deep and secret plotting. Always there reigns a bedlam of noise of pounding machines and clatter of telegraph instruments. Ever and anon an unwary Trencherman will stroll by the casino and be promptly seized by one of the bandits, who then tries to get his prey off to one side and ply him with liquid refreshment. Those unlucky enough not to have a prisoner look with hungry eyes on their more fortunate fellow.

Once a day these outlaws march in serried ranks to confer with Marvin Jones, the Great Pooh Bah and Chief of Staff. They are like bearers of a flag of truce— eyes front and no snooping now!... and there is a soldier at your side to see you obey. Shortly they come marching back, solemnly digesting the orders of the day.

There is an excellent cast of characters playing the minor parts, such as the Indian potentate who plays golf in a sleeveless jersey, his head swathed in a huge white turban and his silky beard enclosed in a hairnet so as not to disturb his putting. (Remember the elastics the gals used to use to keep their skirts from interfering with a swing?) He hits a mighty swat on the course and when he gets in demands a "whiskey and soda" in the most approved theatrical Oxford accent.

There are dark-faced comedians from Ethiopia. One fat and jovial one, blacker than a blackout in the Pennsylvania Station, I feel confident will put on an act which will be a wow. In spite of excess avoirdupois, he can no doubt dance. A little skinny one, even blacker, is his stooge. The latter's blank, dull countenance, which would preclude his employment as a bellboy as lacking intelligence, is no doubt a foil. This pair should be watched for a performance of superior merit. They are champing at the bit to go on, for they, first of all the Trenchermen, wanted to step out and sought to arrange for a dinner to be given at the Cascades Inn. Unfortunately the staff there was too busy caring for the Stanley McGraws and Mary Brooks who had to leave The Homestead, to accommodate them.

The stage is set for a divertissement in the way of bedroom farce. More is yet to come but there was real wit and humor when Sir K. Lee, a typical stage Englishman, on registering, was sent by one clerk to Room 1720, while another sent K. Lee, a smart-looking Chinese, to the same room. It is hard to say which gave the best performance but perhaps the Englishman played the character part more artistically.

Further developments along the same line are promised for Room 517, where the State Department list has located three comely stenographers, one foreign attache, and a runner from the State Department.

Apparently the Russians do not take as readily to light comedy as some others. A lean and cadaverous Cassius refused to allow capitalistic porters to take charge of his baggage, particularly a massive typewriter and a large bag which gurgled. (An F. B. I. man, who came in without knowledge of the State Department, assured me it was not an infernal machine.) One of these articles was to be deposited in his office, the other in his sleeping quarters. He could speak no English and essayed to converse with one of the grounds laborers, pressed into duty as an emergency porter, by sign language. The laborer put on the best part of the act when the dam finally broke and a flood of Russian burst forth.

Three Russian and two Belgian girls who had been forgotten turned up. No rooms for them and they spent most of the night in the Powder Room. Looking at them I came to the conclusion that they had been tried out for the chorus but found inadequate for the part. Probably someone took pity on their disappointment and let them come along as supernumeraries.

Quite a good march act was put on the first night, when ten laborers paraded the length of the lobby in single file, each carrying an unwieldy and obviously heavy box on his shoulders. The boxes were labeled Haig and Veuve Cliquot. The march was well ordered but, on the whole, the act needs rehearsing. This was offered by the South American contingent.

Some of the "sets" are most effective; the long, green baize-covered table in the tower lobby, with forty-four chairs before it, and in front of each chair a small table standard with the name of a sovereign nation upon it; the Empire Room, with elaborate stage, equipped with ramps in case a visitor cannot readily negotiate steps, and other platforms for broadcasting equipment and loud-speakers.

The properties used in the production are magnificent. All the 100 and 200 floor rooms are set up as offices so that each delegate can have at least one secretary—some have more. These are equipped with the finest solid walnut desks which ever graced the halls of The Homestead. On these rest typewriters and dictaphones, obviously just off the manufacturers' shelves. But the management winces when, walking by an open door, a clerk, male or female, is seen sunk in thought, with head resting comfortably against a freshly finished wall surface—and many of them use pomade—or in the next room a red fingernail carelessly flicks the burning ash of a cigarette onto a new carpet.

Some aspects of the production are disappointing. The actors were not carefully enough selected for their parts; they have not been sufficiently drilled or the make-up men were not skillful. Whatever the reason, the spectator gets little impression of purposeful intelligence; certainly there is less in evidence than there was just a year ago when the National Association of Electrical Manufacturers met at The Homestead. The general appearance is decidedly mediocre.

While all this goes on, the soldiers, picked men all, are not unmindful of their biological duty to raise the caliber of the population of Bath County, in which effort they are meeting the heartiest cooperation.

\* \* \* \* \* \*

If we are going to continue the story of the Trencher-men in the same vein in which it was commenced, I suppose the first grand scene was the cocktail party, at which I was not present, followed that night by the first plenary session, where I was allowed and which was sufficiently theatrical. The Empire Room was set up with five hundred and sixty-seven chairs and at one end a long speakers' table with the flags of forty-five nations draped behind it. Two great searchlights, flanking a movie camera of professional size and several smaller machines, were mounted on a raised platform at the edge of the alcove with a similar battery of machines and lights on another at the east end of the room. During the whole of the proceedings press photographers were wandering about with small cameras, each with its own flashlight attachment. In addition to practically continuous exposure of movie film, hundreds of individual photos were being made.

The proceedings of the meeting itself were a burlesque on the democratic process. Jones presided as the temporary chairman, which was natural enough, and immediately suggested that the Conference organize. Rules and regulations had been suggested by an Executive Committee but on the floor of the meeting there was no discussion. It was proposed and seconded that these be adopted, and carried by viva voce vote. Then Jones asked for nominations for the permanent chairman and someone nominated him. A Dutchman could hardly wait to second the nomination. After a few minutes of silence Jones declared the nominations closed and had himself elected by viva voce vote. There was no pretense of a deliberative assembly.

Jones then read Roosevelt's letter of welcome. It was in the President's best vein. It might be studied for months without gaining a hint as to what concrete action was expected. After this, Jones made his speech of welcome.

I suppose when a man talks of famine and sudden death in war, and you are acutely conscious that both are present and near, no speech can be said to be banal. Jones' diction, voice and mannerisms were all in the most approved fresh-water college tradition. The desire to have the have-nots of the world's population get more has been voiced *ad nauseam* in speeches to assemblies and over radios. It has been written about by everyone who has published a book on world economics during the last twenty years. The same holds true for the panacea of cooperation. These were the keynotes of Jones' speech. Nothing novel was said nor were the old platitudes presented more effectively or beautifully than had been done a thousand times before. The speech had two merits. It was not unduly long, I should say not half an hour, and the enunciation excellent so all he said could be heard.

He was followed by D. Kuo, a Chinese. This man wandered away from the mike and I got but fragments of what he said. It was clearly the speech of an educated man, using English as spoken in these United States, perfectly idiomatic and without a trace of foreign accent. The scraps I heard carried conviction and intelligence. I should like to have followed more closely the comparatively short passages dealing with Kuo's unhappy country.

After Kuo, Jones pulled a Rotary Club trick by asking the members of the various delegations to stand *seriatim* so they could be made known to their fellows. One noticed the loud applause for the Russians, French and smaller fighting countries and only polite claps for the English. Then the Star Spangled Banner was sung and the Conference commenced.

# 26. Vale

WITH the end of the Food Conference, life in the Valley returned to something like normal and dramatics were over for The Homestead. Business came back until, as in the twenties, it seemed that everyone and his wife wanted to come here. Now the modernization of the hotel could go forward without the limitations of money shortages. Throughout the hard years of the depression the properties had been maintained, but really only in status quo. There had been nothing left over with which to improve equipment or

buildings in keeping with the general advance of standards
but now that became possible. Almost at once a completely modern kitchen was built and much done in
the way of new decorations where the old, if sound,
had become outmoded.

At the same time, in spite of taxes, burdensome
largely because the reorganization under the Bank-
ruptcy Act had left the Company with a hopelessly inadequate tax base for calculating excess profits tax, the
financial position of the Company improved and it became possible in 1948 to correct the evils of the corporate
structure of 1940. The first step was the elimination of
the holdings of the Chesapeake and Ohio Railway, then
the elimination of the mortgages with their burdensome
restrictions.

This brings us down to modern times. Looking back
over almost sixty years, the Valley Road seems much the
same as when first I saw it in the early nineties, at least
when away from the conventional and immediate. A
few days ago, on the way back from the airport, I stopped
at the lookout on Keyser's Rock and let my eyes roam
over the landscape. The Road wound in and out of
copses, meandering from one side of the Valley to the
other, glistening silver gray instead of the bright yellow
in the days of clay surface. A few more houses were apparent but the wooded ridges, fading into the blue, were
unchanged. Far off in the distance, over the West Virginia line, the fire tower at High Point on Alleghany
Mountain was hardly a discordant note, so hazy and in-
distinct it was. An Indian standing there before the days
of Columbus would have seen about what I did; even the
little clearing on top of Cole's Mountain might have been
there, a sort of mountain park. He would have seen the
blackjack oak, with its shriveled brown leaves, in the

early fall and the ground cover of purple blueberry bushes splashed with the vivid green of high altitude rhododendron. The strength and beauty of the ridges near and far, their rounded shoulders stretching down toward the Valley like mighty buttresses, must have impressed him in the silence so intense he could hear the late crickets chirp the treble to the low hum of a land passing into autumn. He, as I, could forget the irritations of busybody fellow men and merge into the tranquillity of the Peaceful Valley.

9 781163 819586